Shots to the Heart: For the Love of Film Performance

Shots to the Heart: For the Love of Film Performance

Steven Rybin

Anthem Impacts
London

ANTHEM PRESS

Anthem Press
An imprint of Wimbledon Publishing Company
www.anthempress.com

This edition first published in UK and USA 2022
by ANTHEM PRESS
75–76 Blackfriars Road, London SE1 8HA, UK
or PO Box 9779, London SW19 7ZG, UK
and
244 Madison Ave #116, New York, NY 10016, USA

British Library Cataloguing-in-Publication Data
A catalogue record for this book is available from the British Library.

Library of Congress Cataloging-in-Publication Data
A catalog record for this book has been requested.

ISBN-13: 978-1-83998-591-1 (Pbk)
ISBN-10: 1-83998-591-7 (Pbk)

This title is also available as an e-book.

CONTENTS

Acknowledgments		vi
1.	Making an Entrance	1
2.	A Little Notepad	7
3.	Androgynous Eyes	13
4.	A Human Something	21
5.	Gesture and Desire	27
6.	Broken Glass	35
7.	A Way of Moving	41
8.	A Glint of Deathlessness	47
9.	Possible Stars	51
10.	A Little Love	55
11.	In Any Other Pair of Eyes	61
Notes		69
Index		75

ACKNOWLEDGMENTS

I thank the acquisitions and editing team at Anthem Press for their support of this project, especially Kyro Huddleston, Megan Greiving, Courtney Young, and Jebaslin Hephzibah. I also want to thank Sreejith Govindan for assistance with the copyediting. I thank the peer reviewers of the text who graciously helped me improve the book (of course, any remaining flaws are all mine). This book is dedicated to Jessica Belser, my favorite moviegoing companion.

There are faces that subjugate one, that are turned away from
with a feeling like that of giving up breath itself.

—James Salter[1]

Between one actor's tricks of intonation and inflection and another's,
the most trifling differences would strike me as being of an incalculable
importance.

—Marcel Proust[2]

Chapter 1

MAKING AN ENTRANCE

Everything about falling for an actor seems obvious. But nothing about it is.

A film lover knows when it happens: the heart beats faster, fluttering alongside the undulations of an actor's gestures, movements, voice. These feelings have parallels in experiences outside the cinema, in everyday lives, when someone's way of moving and speaking fascinates or beguiles. The eye knows intuitively when it is charmed—every eye has its types, people who enthrall and surprise, in films as in life. This is not only pleasure. In the cinema, at least, it also involves labor. An actor toils to achieve a performance, and filmmakers work to arrange and orchestrate the actor's effort through mise en scène, framing, and cutting. The actor isn't doing it alone, even as she sometimes seems to be—during those moments of viewing when she overtakes the composition of the film, becoming its dominant, and most human, motif. An actor's overtaking of an eye is an enchantment.[3] And it is the result of a process of behind-the-scenes craft to which the viewer is not directly privy.[4] Putting words to paper to think about performance is also creative work, which may contain in response to the actor's charms some fresh discovery within the viewing self. That lightning flash of sudden affection—fleeting and intense—that a performer in the art of cinema impresses into thought is the subject of this book.

Even actors a viewer knows well can mesmerize in freshly dizzying ways, repeatedly.[5] And this vertigo can be provoked by a very simple movement—an actor's way of entering.

At the beginning of George Cukor's 1932 film *A Bill of Divorcement*, Katharine Hepburn, in her first screen performance, declares her presence, in tandem with a camera that will make clear it knows how to present her. Her command of the screen is especially memorable in Cukor's cinema. In the opening sequence, Cukor begins with a high-angle traveling shot that sweeps gradually over the ground floor of a comfortably accommodated family home. A handsome man (David Manners) is walking through this room, searching. He stops—the camera stopping momentarily with him—at this sofa, and then that table, finding chattering and dancing society people but not the one for whom he pines. He eventually reaches the bottom of a staircase and looks up: his eye catches her now. The camera swivels up. Hepburn floats into the shot and looks down at Manners: her dress is made of sleeveless and flowing white fabric, giving her something like wings, an ethereal reality (Figure 1).

At the beginning of this shot, Cukor keeps the staircase out of frame. Only its diagonal movement reveals this camera to have been up there the entire time, perched near the second floor where Hepburn emerges. The camera's revelation of Manners' discovery of Hepburn walking into the shot is only a pretense, for the camera was already there, waiting for her, ready to admire her entrance, to catch her when she enters the frame, at the moment when she declares herself ready to be caught. The hesitant, stopping-and-starting movement that characterized Manners' initial search for his screen partner now gives way to Hepburn's left-to-right flow as she bounds across the second floor of the house to the other side of the frame, slipping down the stairs to join the party. Hepburn is not merely filmed here by Cukor, but intimately held by his frame, the attention of which she holds in turn; her way of moving and being onscreen defines, for a sliver of screen time, the purpose of the film's existence, a human inflection of the camera's mechanical gaze.

Figure 1: *A Bill of Divorcement* (1932).

In this description, I've not actually mentioned the name of Hepburn's character in *A Bill of Divorcement*. (It's Sydney.) In cinema, characters are often taken for granted; like plot machinations and genre tropes, characters are abstract concepts fallen back upon to explain, after the fact and almost always too quickly, the meaning of a film. Patrice Pavis, in his writing on stage performance, uses the word "vectorization" to describe that invisible, emotional dart thrown from an actor's gesture to a viewing eye. For Pavis, the actor's movements are material experiences: in a stage play, they are born out of the arrangement of people, objects, lighting, and décor; and in cinema, out of a similar arrangement orchestrated for the camera, attuned to rhythms of editing and sound. "When confronted with a gesture, a space, or a piece of music, the spectator should endeavor to appreciate its materiality for *as long as possible*," Pavis writes (emphases throughout this quote are his). "*At first* she will be touched, astonished, or silenced by these things that offer themselves to her, before *later on* they become completely integrated into the rest of the performance and evaporate into an immaterial signified [...] sooner or later, the spectator's desire is bound to be vectorized; the arrow will inevitably reach its target, transforming the object of desire into a signified."[6] For Pavis, the actor's work—the physical, onscreen remnants of it, manifest in the movements of body and inflections of voice preserved in the finished film—produces little, invisible arrows, rendering these stars onscreen as fluttering Cupids, the viewers watching them their targets.

All this emotional quivering in response to a screen performer was once an experience shared by film viewers who felt no need to self-consciously call themselves cinephiles; cinema and the stars who orbited it were a central part of the culture of moving images, and love for cinema in such a culture is not a theoretical concept but a form of life. Roland Barthes nostalgically muses upon such worship in his paean to Greta Garbo, in which he declares that Garbo "still belongs to that moment in cinema when capturing the human face still plunged audiences into the deepest ecstasy, when one literally lost oneself in a human image as one would in a philtre, when the face represented a kind of absolute state of the flesh, which could be neither reached nor renounced."[7] Barthes's essay is a poetic variation on the popular reception of movie stars, akin to the sprawling writings of the French Impressionist critics of the late 1910s and early 1920s. Such rapture, indicative of the capacity for cinema to generate the emotional experience Pavis discusses, is especially intense in the writings of Jean Epstein, whose love for the actor's body and its capabilities is emblemized by this ardent celebration of Sessue Hayakawa:

The Honor of His House [1918] is an improbable yarn: adultery and surgery. Hayakawa, the tranced tragedian, sweeps the scenario aside.

A few instants offer the magnificent sight of his harmony in movement. He crosses a room quite naturally, his torso held at a slight angle. He hands his gloves to a servant. Opens a door. Then, having gone out, closes it. *Photogénie*, pure *photogénie*, cadenced movement.[8]

Epstein, admiring Hayakawa's sweeping of the storyline aside with a single gesture, a pose, a movement, performs a similar feat in his writing, darting past any concern for that "improbable yarn" in favor of "a few instants" that offer "the magnificent sight" of Hayakawa's "harmony in movement."

What Epstein adores of Hayakawa onscreen are everyday behaviors, performed by a particular body—how he crosses the room, the way he holds his torso. But these are stylized gestures of normal behavior, delectable manifestations of presence emerging from, even as they move beyond, a narrative, with narrative form serving as a cinematic proscenium within which the actor, lifting off from within it, creates another reality. Epstein's writing on Hayakawa goes beyond plot to form a connoisseurship, a collected remembrance of fleeting physical impressions inscribed on celluloid, gathered and arranged in memory. Without reducing his appreciation of Hayakawa to an illustration of a theory, Epstein nevertheless takes very seriously the concept of *photogénie*, an elusive notion referring to the poetic beauty the cinema both bestows upon and extracts from the people and objects it films.[9] *Photogénie* is related to but means more than "photogenic": as Epstein's description of Hayakawa's movements makes clear, *photogénie*, in an experience of film performance, also refers to a way of moving, and a way for the viewer to be held by movement, the very viewer who in turn tries to hold onto the way she was held by the actor through words, even as performance slips always away from the eye as the film moves ineluctably on.[10]

The fleeting fascinations Barthes glimpsed in Garbo's face and Epstein luxuriated in as he watched Hayakawa move are worth taking seriously. But often these little darts the actors throw go uncaught, as viewers jump straight to accounts of the plot or discussions of how expectations were or were not fulfilled by a movie. Pavis, in the quote mentioned earlier, asks us to slow down a bit, as Barthes and Epstein do, to linger upon these performers, to share a space—of viewing, and of writing—languorously with them; and to share a set of minutes with them, a duration that, irrespective of the attempts of some scholars to quantify things like "average shot lengths," is all the more elusive given that it is never, as felt experience, exactly measurable.

Pavis also implies a distinction, and temporal distance, between the prelinguistic affect, or emotion, generated in us by a performance— the way we are moved by an actor—and the linguistic signified generated by that experience. But in firmly distinguishing between and to some extent separating these two different aspects of performance's appreciation, Pavis might also be leaping too quickly over the space that exists in-between them, the ways that being moved by an actor continue to happen as one writes, and also as one reads that writing, and connects that reading to other moments and memories of performance. I am not so sure the experience of a moving performance, or the languid ways we find of being with actors as they move, can be quite so cleanly separated from an act of writing which itself seeks languorousness, which seeks to linger and allow a moment with the actor to last a little longer. What was felt, what was intoxicating about the performer, what we discovered while watching her but also while pining for the performative magic to last just a little longer, should slip into the writing, should not be fully dissolved into a sober signified. The actor's heartbeat, which in cinematic experience is only ever really the heartbeat of performance as felt by the viewer, should, ideally, live on a little in the words and the sentences placed on the page.

Chapter 2

A LITTLE NOTEPAD

In Alan Rudolph's 1976 film *Welcome to L.A.*, Geraldine Chaplin plays Karen Hood, a housewife who spends her days riding around in taxi cabs, imitating Greta Garbo. Her love for Garbo could belong to the same pantheon as Sal Mineo's quiet affection for Alan Ladd in *Rebel Without a Cause* (Nicholas Ray, 1955) or Constance Bennett's playful flirtation with a magazine photo of Clark Gable in *What Price Hollywood?* (George Cukor, 1932). But this is a remarkable case in which a character's love for an actor emerges from the actor's own: according to Rudolph, the idea that her character would imitate Garbo was Chaplin's.[11]

In *Welcome to L.A.*, Chaplin shapes Karen as a character who uses performance to imagine a more satisfying life. Her self-styled personal drama eventually finds an audience in Carroll Barber (Keith Carradine), a playboy songwriter in Los Angeles to attend new studio recordings of his songs. Carradine first encounters Chaplin sitting on a curb on a quiet street. As he drives up, she's jotting something down in her notepad—Karen is a writer, of the most private kind, and the words she speaks, sometimes to other characters but also sometimes in a direct address to the camera, are quite arcane, as if she were conducting an experiment in the ability of words to describe an emotional state, as if her text were still in the process of being worked-out even as she speaks it. She is wearing the same red beret and fur coat she always wears as she travels around Los Angeles. But here, for a moment, she rests; killing time, writing. Barber is curious, so he pulls up beside her. Rudolph frames much of their conversation from the passenger side of the car, as Carradine looks out the window at Chaplin (Figure 2). Carradine asks if she wants a ride. Karen pretends not to hear, and then, bringing her eyes to his, claims she can't go with him because she can't drive. Karen, rather than communicate soberly, prefers instead to perform, sliding into her Garbo cough—again an homage to the film she adores, *Camille* (George Cukor, 1936)—as she looks back down at her notepad.

"I've just been to a movie and I was the only person there," she tells him. "It's nice when you're by yourself," Carradine suggests. Karen is not sure if it is nice. "Well—men always have a better time," she answers; "Maybe it's because they understand the situation." Rudolph cuts to a shot of Carradine, inside the car; Barber is now carefully contemplating her words—she is saying more than she had a good time at the movies. *Camille* is a part of her, and she would have liked to have had someone with her there to share the emotions radiating from the screen on which it was projected, perhaps precisely just as she felt them. Here, as Carradine lingers on Chaplin's words, Chaplin's Karen is performing Garbo mannerisms so as to hold onto the passions of *Camille* that she caught while watching it; this is the embodied equivalent of the notepad and pen, the creation of one performance holding onto something glimpsed in another. She continues coughing; he offers her a drink from his whisky bottle, extending this moment of encounter but also trying to help her out with her cough—maybe he wants to get rid of that cough so he can find out who Karen Hood really is. But she insists on, persists with, Garbo; the drink has merely improved her performance of coughing. "It was so sad when she died at the end," Karen reports; "she said—*Nanine* [...] *Nanine* [...]" As Chaplin cries for Marguerite's maid, Carradine watches, bemused.

Chaplin does not imitate Garbo to suggest that her character is masking her real self from others; there is here no essential self hidden behind creative gesture and self-conscious social presentation. Her Garbo is her own, as true to her "real self" as anything else (and different from Barthes's Garbo, given that Chaplin is more obsessed with the voice than the face of the screen goddess). This attempt by Chaplin's character to incarnate a performance—in part, through writing (she is nearly always in this film equipped with her notepad)— is a kind of mechanism she uses, in the world of the story, to alternately draw Carradine close and then push him away, finally only fantasizing about rather than actualizing a possible affair. Chaplin embodies here a dialectic of revealing and concealing, and of using a memory of a screen performance as a source of creative energy, using Garbo as an inspiration to orient herself in a world of gesture, emotion, and thought.

Figure 2: *Welcome to L.A.* (1976).

An impressive body of work in film studies takes unabashed pleasure in movies, seeking not to rest with that pleasure but rather to use it as a generative force for criticism. A lot of this writing was for a time mobilized, in a self-consciously theoretical way, in the name of "cinephilia." It is striking to see how so much of this English-language scholarship flirts with actors, without ever quite committing to them. Robert B. Ray's 2001 book *How a Film Theory Got Lost, or Other Mysteries in Cultural Studies*—one of my first personal encounters, in the year before I began my own study of film in a graduate program, with academic writing on film—calls for the film scholar to think again about *photogénie*, that striking and elusive quality of photographic-based cinema flickering behind Epstein's descriptions of Hayakawa and other stars, a quality of life the camera soaks in as it witnesses some slice of arranged reality before it.[12] As Ray notes, this fascination often results in a writer's "acute description of the way movies are often experienced—as intermittent intensities (a face, a landscape, the fall of light across a room)."[13] Ray explores a fascination for cinema generated by *photogénie*, with the actor playing a salient role in much of his writing (he writes much of interest about Jimmy Stewart, Katharine Hepburn, and other actors in his recent work).[14] Later work that manifests sensibilities similar to Ray's, by contrast, tends to shift the actor to a supporting role. Christian Keathley's 2006 study *Cinephilia and History, or the Wind in the Trees* is animated by the "revelatory potential" of a film lover's engagement with cinema, wherein a fleeting detail of image or sound—the rustling of leaves in the wind, the blink of an eye, bright red lipstick on Natalie Wood's lips—becomes enduringly fascinating, above and beyond the importance of these fragments to narrative.[15] Other writers take up this idea of the fleeting moment of cinema and apply it in different ways, and in relation to different formations of cinematic pleasure. Rashna Wadia Richards has written on the traces of affecting contingency she finds coursing through Classical Hollywood cinema (supporting actors in this fascination include Fred Astaire and Orson Welles).[16] And a host of writers, in a pair of essay collections edited by Scott Balcerzak and Jason Sperb, explore forms of film love engendered by digital cinema (some of these authors are fascinated by the body's—if not strictly the film actor's—relationship to the digital camera).[17]

These books that circle around a love for film are not centrally about performance. In these writings, the actor is nearly always there, but usually only in a supporting role in descriptions and analyses of other filmic phenomena.

One example of the way the actor often takes on an adjunct role in support of another, larger object of cinematic fascination is illustrated in Keathley's citation of a moment of film pleasure described by the French writer Gilbert Adair, in which Adair is in thrall not so much to Cary Grant but to the socks Cary Grant wears in the crop-duster sequence from Alfred Hitchcock's *North by Northwest* (1959).[18] Adair's fascination with Grant's socks is with their novelty, the sense that these marginal moments are unique to this particular, discerning film viewer's attention, in contrast to what is assumed to be the plot-focused attention of the average moviegoer. (This is essentially equivalent to my own suggestion, expressed earlier in these pages, that viewers tend to leap to abstract conceptions of "character" without lingering on the performance itself.) This distinction between ways of viewing—the presumed cinephile's attention to marginalia or unexpected, contingent surprises, as opposed to a fixation on the presumably intended arrangement of plot, genre expectation, and character psychology—perhaps explains why the actor is less frequently the central focus in scholarly writings on film pleasure. Everyone who goes to the movies loves actors: Cary Grant was one of the most popular stars of his era, and one does not have to be a cinephile to fall for him. A fixation on Grant, in other words, is not going to win a movie lover any measure of social distinction or cultural capital—the acknowledgement of a refined taste unique to the connoisseur, displayed in the twenty-first-century, most often, in forms of carefully curated social media postings[19]—since at the movie theater every "slow Joe in the back row" (to quote David Bordwell's phrase for the perhaps less-than-average moviegoer) presumably loves the stars populating the screen.[20]

For more than a few serious lovers of film, stars and actors are even something of an impediment to a properly cultivated love of the cinema. Gazing hopelessly at stars, for some, seems to be simply not a distinctive enough activity, precisely because presumably everybody does it: and because everybody does it, star gazing threatens to obscure the more fine-grained, distinguished attention of the cineaste. "Cinephilia," after all, is often about looking for those exciting, marginal, fleeting moments in films that "normal" viewers, hungry for narrative and genre, miss. Liz Czach, for example, commenting on the celebrity-dominated context of major film festivals, pointedly argues that "the cinephiliac moment cannot, and never could [...] compete with a star event. It is, then, little wonder that the largely invisible cinephiliac experience appears to be under threat from the largely visible star culture, an atmosphere wherein the stargazer's 'Who did you see?' replaces the cinephile's 'What did you see?'".[21] But I suggest there need be no incommensurability between a serious love for movies and the little darts actors throw at us. Following this line of thinking, I prefer instead to understand characters in film narratives as the accumulated outcome of the movie lover's affectionate appreciation of a performance and its various gestures, movements, and expressions. Lingering around a moment of performance cannot, of course, forestall the forward momentum of a movie which always eventually engulfs the moment; but such lingering may nevertheless provide a way of returning to moments (to rescue actors and their gestures from the surging tides and heaving floods of narrative, as it were), and a way of acknowledging the role actors play in the time we spend living with the cinema.

This understanding takes work, however, and as Czach's discussion implies, requires some distinction between a frozen, utterly besotted, and fixed gaze upon the performer and a more creative and writerly engagement moved by enchantment and dynamic subjectivity. As I've suggested, simply noticing a film actor will not be enough to distinguish the connoisseur's loving attention toward film. The actor is to be remembered, cherished, written about, lived with. Geraldine Chaplin's character in *Welcome to L.A.* is, in this respect, a remarkable and unpretentious lover of film performance, for she does not simply notice but attends to and remembers Garbo. Chaplin lives with, and reincarnates, Garbo's performance in her own form of life—her ways of speaking, moving, gesturing, and languidly passing the time in a creative way. This goes beyond obsession and fixation with, a hopeless gaze upon, a particular star and toward a fresh incarnation of that screen figure in waking life, and in writing. For Chaplin, her little notepad always in tow in *Welcome to L.A.*, Garbo is not a "star icon" whose meaning is complete and engraved in an already-existing culture industry but rather an ongoingly moving presence in films, a particular manifestation of voice and gesture who might in turn shape the voice and gesture of those who adore her. And nor does Chaplin's love for film require a self-consciously theoretical cinephilia. She requires only her viewing self and its attendant history of desires. "When we consider performances that have touched and provoked us," Murray Pomerance writes, "we call up biography, memory, desire, feeling, and orientation—in short, the self."[22] We often fear the self, and are taught, if not to avoid entirely the "I" in academic writing, to abstract it in "discourse," to shape it into a fully socialized and instrumental object that can flow with immediate legibility and currency in rhetorical and cultural waters. But the "I" is ultimately the one who performs—or, the "I" is the one generated out of a performance—and cannot be avoided if one is to write meaningfully about experiences of acting.

Chaplin teaches us this, too: her self in *Welcome to L.A.* is not one that precedes performance but which is rather perpetually generated by the various ways in which it becomes capable of, alternately, emotional projection and reception, for how it looks through and beyond narrative to glimpse longingly at gesture and movement, ways of moving and seeing that she might in turn embody. Narrative and genre threaten to turn us into dutiful, repetitive consumers; gesture and movement move us forward with human passion and unpredictability, prompting existentially ambiguous reflections upon desire. Chaplin's way of looking at Garbo does not remain settled with the plot of *Camille*, and does not attempt to politely block the effects the performances she has seen have had on her "I" who speaks. That is where her distinction is won: not in her wielding of some preformulated way of seeing Garbo, but in her own inventive and lively existence alongside and through Garbo, her own performance. Chaplin's character inscribes the little darts the actor throws at her on her notepad and in her life, and then gifts a few of them, in her distinctive variation, to her own viewers.

Chapter 3

ANDROGYNOUS EYES

Keisuke Kinoshita's film *The Girl I Loved* (1946) is beautifully attentive to its performers: it sees them not only as people playing characters, but also as generative contributors to a cinematic tapestry. Kinoshita's cinema looks at people with languorous attentiveness, not possessive but lingering, open to the continual challenge of gesture and movement, and to the possibility of performance to create rhymes with the film's own movements and gestures. In one sequence, Kuniko Igawa (Figure 3), playing a young woman named Yoshiko, is washing up after a day of work, cleaning her face, and changing her dress, a transition from her character's workday in her rural village to something more interior, a little more private. After spying something on the top shelf as she goes about this business, Igawa looks outside. She then grabs a small suitcase from the shelf. Kinoshita cuts to a long shot of Igawa taken from an opposite angle outside the house, as she runs out of the house and toward the other side. As Igawa runs, Kinoshita slows the framerate slightly—he will do this for poetic effect at various junctures throughout the film—and throws the middle and background out of focus, which renders Igawa's temporarily slowed movement toward the camera very like a dream; she eventually drifts closer to the camera, ending the shot in a focused close-up (and in a framerate restored to normal speed) as she removes a dress from the small case. Here it is the actor's movement, and not the camera, which creates a change in shot distance, giving the performer pride of place in the gradual unfolding and modulation of mise en scène and the frame. But it is also the effect of the camera, and here of its shallow focus, to fetishize the movement of the body toward the lens even as Igawa herself remains, for a moment, slightly blurry, visually inaccessible. Kinoshita's, and our, attention is then diverted for a moment to the dress, which once belonged to her mother, and which Yoshiko plans to wear the day she gets married. She hooks the dress to a tree branch to air it out; shadows of the dress and of the branches play across her face. After this, Kinoshita cuts to a long shot, from a reverse angle, showing Igawa and a line of trees against a horizon line, the dress blowing in the wind.

Now arrives Jirô (Norio Ôtsuka), a young villager, curious about Igawa, and the dress. He asks where it came from. It is the dress, belonging to her late mother, that Yoshiko was wrapped in after she was abandoned by her parents. At this, Igawa wraps the dress around her body, imitating the infant she was while at the same time showing us the woman she is becoming. The character sees in this dress the memory of her mother. Kinoshita sees Igawa, in turn, as the onscreen equivalent of his own camera's way of being in the world, as it seeks to wrap itself up in texture and movement, in moments that linger on people and their fascination with things. For a moment, though, it is Jirô who is Kinoshita's onscreen surrogate, a male in this world fascinated by feminine fabric: after Yoshiko leaves the frame to go back inside, Jirô playfully wraps himself up in the dress, twirling about in it before following her to the door. "It must make the woman who wears it look like a heavenly maiden," Jirô says; "That's right," Yoshiko agrees, her attention diverted to makeup and a mirror, "My mother is dancing in heaven." Jirô offers to play his harmonica for Yoshiko's mother, and as he begins his music Kinoshita cuts to two shots of the dress blowing in the wind, as if dancing, and then to a shot of Jirô playing, from which point the camera pans to Igawa, gesturing to her face with a powder puff. Kinoshita will then cut to a close shot of Igawa, her gesture with the puff rhythmically timed to the music, and then to cutaway shots returning us, now closer, to the dress dancing in the wind, and then back to a pair of closer shots of Igawa, bringing lipstick to her lips. This dance of cutting now increases in speed, Kinoshita's usual languorousness replaced momentarily by quicker rhythms. And yet this change in pace is just another form of lingering, like a strolling dandy who only momentarily becomes intensely interested in something on offer in a shop display. The film shuttles us back and forth from close shots of the dress to close shots of Igawa adjusting her eyebrows and combing her hair. Each time we see Igawa, and the dancing dress, it is from a slightly different angle, as if Kinoshita were searching for all the various possibilities and positions from which one might look at Igawa but also the dress, which Kinoshita's camera and cutting is investing with new life and movement. The effect is to make Igawa part of the film's tapestry, inflecting her gestures and expressions with details from the world surrounding her and with the editing which links her to that world; but it is also to allow the film's gradual unfolding to be inflected and changed by Igawa's presence. Kinoshita's film seeks to create something, or to turn itself into something, in dedication to her: a cinema that is itself like the dancing dress, imbued by Kinoshita's camera with new life.

Figure 3: *The Girl I Loved* (1946).

Writers on film pride themselves on finding auteurs where there were no auteurs before. Chris Fujiwara has suggested that the privileging of many marginal Classical Hollywood films by lovers of the cinema is motivated by a sense that "the work, having been deformed by commercial and ideological pressures and perhaps abandoned or taken away from its author, now remains to be completed by its viewer, whom its imperfections and incoherences invite to assume the role of collaborator."[23] The protective cherishing of maligned or ignored films by passionate viewers reminds me of French New Wave filmmaker Jacques Rivette's reverence for the cinema of Nicholas Ray, whose work in Hollywood for Rivette required "a little love"[24] from the viewer to compensate for the misdirected devaluation it received from many critics.

All this is to say that a similar compensatory love might also be at play in the affection of film viewers, and perhaps some auteurs themselves, for actors. We have already glimpsed Barthes's fascination with Greta Garbo, and Epstein's admiration of Sessue Hayakawa. In my description of *The Girl I Loved*, I've begun to suggest how Keisuke Kinoshita—a director who could use a little more attention in film studies—mobilizes a fascination with Kuniko Igawa that propels the rhythms of the entire scene, a fascination with an actor extending also to male performers in his cinema: Kinoshita puts into play a way of looking that I would describe as androgynous, open to the fascination any figure onscreen might generate. But both Garbo and Hayakawa were already beloved by legions; what is also part of a love for film is the discovery of performers, a way of seeing set into motion by actors not so well known.

Louise Brooks might be the supreme exemplar of this phenomenon in the history of cinema. A contract player in Hollywood during the late 1920s, Brooks in U.S. cinema is most notable for her role as a lithe, playful circus diver in the early Howard Hawks film *A Girl in Every Port* (1928) and as a runaway drifter who dresses in boy's clothing in William A. Wellman's *Beggars of Life* (1928). Despite the function the Brooks character plays in these films in a love triangle involving two other men, Brooks in both films strikes an androgynous figure, particularly in her character's predilection for masculine clothing in the Wellman film. And yet audiences of the time took little note of Brooks's presence or her play with gender, and little notice too of the now-legendary films she made for G.W. Pabst in Europe, *Pandora's Box* (1928) and *Diary of a Lost Girl* (1929).

And so Brooks and her tomboyish femininity had to be seen by a discerning eye, as she indeed was, and not shortly after the future critics of *Cahiers du cinéma* in France were claiming hitherto marginal names such as Hawks and Nicholas Ray as major figures of cinema. Key to the rediscovery of Brooks in later decades was the director of the Cinémathèque Française, Henri Langlois, who wrapped these loving words around her: "She is the intelligence of the cinematic process, of all that is photogenic; she embodies all that the cinema rediscovered in the last years of the silent film: complete naturalness, and complete simplicity."[25] Kenneth Tynan, another of those critics smitten by Brooks, wrote upon seeing *Pandora's Box* for the third time: "Infatuation with L. Brooks reinforced by second viewing of *Pandora*. She has run through my life like a magnetic thread—this shameless urchin tomboy, this unbroken, unbreakable porcelain filly."[26] If Tynan's besotted declaration veers (rather delightfully, I think) toward camp, it is notable that Brooks herself anticipated the emotional tenor her belated reception would take in one of her own performances, three decades earlier. In her third and final film in Europe, Augusto Genina's fascinating *Prix de Beauté* (1930), Brooks plays Lucienne, a winner of a local beauty contest who earns a part in a film. Her husband, jealous of her desire to become an actress, trails Lucienne into a projection room where her forthcoming movie is being previewed. Shot dead by this cad, Brooks performs her character's fall before us as Lucienne's diegetic performance, recorded some time before this tragic affair, continues flickering on the screen behind her. In this moment, Brooks herself performatively prefigures her own celebrity afterlife in cinema, long after her brief Hollywood and European film career had passed, indeed long after she died.

Cinephilia as an academic discourse is often characterized by its necrophiliac undertones—that is, for its obsession with a projected filmic image of a long-dead past.[27] But I am more interested in the ways in which devotees of the cinema, through their besotted eyes, themselves perform their own enchanting acts of magic: bringing actors back to life, in writing, even at times in the making of films themselves.[28] A filmmaker who has woven this love for a cherished, marginalized performer into the work of cinema itself is Joseph Cornell, whose film *Rose Hobart* (1936) remains the shining exemplar of performative fixation in all cinema. Cornell, an artist and experimental filmmaker, purchased a print of the 1931 Universal programmer *East of Borneo* from a warehouse that was discarding reels of films on 16mm. With the use of his personal editing machine, Cornell spliced together fragments of Hobart's performance from *East of Borneo* together with shots of an eclipse taken from a documentary. In *East of Borneo*, Hobart plays a woman who goes searching for her husband on the exotic island of the film's title, becoming in turn an object of desire of the island's prince (Georges Renavent). Cornell indulges in a like form of desire in his film, fetishizing Hobart's gestures and movements by recontextualizing them in a filmic context that enables them to slip away from the very narrative machinations which initially framed the performance. In this, Cornell sees the actor not as a function of cinema; he sees the actor *as cinema*, a moving figure whose quivering, when placed into dialogue with other rhythms, becomes generative and mysterious rather than predetermined and functional.

And yet Cornell's desire goes beyond, and is more interesting than, the prince's lusting after Hobart's character in the narrative of *East of Borneo*. Through his displacement of Hobart's performance, Cornell emphasizes her qualities that resist and transcend the plot of the source film. Cornell's attentive gaze wrests Hobart away from *East of Borneo*; her performance, in terms of its photographically captured details, is the same in the Cornell film, but now other qualities of her person and being become palpable. As Deborah Solomon writes:

And like much of Cornell's future work, the movie is an idealized portrait of a female performer. It makes us feel the emotions that come with being a fan: Rose Hobart looms before us as an icon. Yet her appeal is not purely feminine. With her short hair and slender, flat frame, Rose Hobart is a study in androgyny, the first of many boyish girls to surface in Cornell's work. We first see her dressed in a man's jacket and tie; later she appears in a silky evening dress—her masculine and feminine costumes blurring the boundaries of gender.[29]

This playful sexuality is already percolating in *East of Borneo* before Cornell gets to it, a film in which Hobart wears a mix of "masculine and feminine costumes."

But as Solomon implies, Hobart's movements are only foregrounded as such once the narrative trappings of the original film have been discarded, and once Cornell has resituated Hobart in a rhythmic structure free to appreciate her alluring, feminine boyishness, her gestures, and her movements. In its playful attention to the way in which a performance has the potential to slip away from normative definitions of social being and comportment, Cornell's film confirms something I have always felt to be true—at least potentially—about the film lover's devotion to favorite performers: that this devotion, at heart, desires something like a fulsome androgyny in the fragments that it collects, an in-betweenness that is perhaps driven by a particular object of desire—an actor—but that also has the potential to color an entire film, and the way one moves and thinks through it. There are many studies of androgyny in cinema, and of the ensuing ambiguity it has the power to spark in screen narrative; but to conceptualize a way of looking at and desire for performance as itself androgynous, as refusing to define its nature of fascination as finally either male or female, is a fresh welcoming of the range of gestures and expressions actors in films give us. These little intimacies dart past normative or socially articulated definitions of identity and ask us for something rather more generative, a quality of reception that is as open to forgetting its social position and place as it is to asserting it.

In Cornell's film, Rose Hobart is an example of a Hollywood player in whom something neither rigidly male nor female is seen, something worth placing up there again on a screen and wondering more about. Hobart did not become the legend Louise Brooks became, but her conjuring in the Cornell film parallels the infatuation of Langlois and Tynan with Brooks. In both cases, lovers of cinema attach themselves to actors who were only bit players in the commerce of the Hollywood star system, and their affection leads to a recontextualization of the performer in another context: in the case of Brooks, a renewed appreciation within film culture for her work in Europe for G.W. Pabst, and in the case of Hobart, the resituating of her performances and her images in experimental cinema and the art world.

A love for film performance, in its desire for something other than already-articulated identities, could also focus on sharing affectionate descriptions of bit players or less well-known stars one has glimpsed across a lifetime of film watching, names not so well recognized by the public but which have made themselves felt across a life's viewings. In a 2001 dossier of essays devoted to the female star in cinema, Joe McElhaney writes eloquently of Bess Flowers, a frequently uncredited bit player who is a moving presence, for those equipped to see her, in scores of Hollywood movies. McElhaney introduces Flowers in his essay in grand fashion, declaring to the reader that "She has appeared in more great films than any actor, male or female, in all of American cinema, in a career that encompassed everything from Chaplin's *A Woman of Paris* (1923) to Hitchcock's *Vertigo* (1958), from silent cinema to sound, from the heyday of the traditional Hollywood studio system to its declining years."[30] And as he goes on to write, "If a fundamental impulse behind cinephilia is to embrace the marginal and elevate the elusive fragment over the whole, what could be more cinephilic than to become fixated on Bess Flowers?"[31] What is most striking in McElhaney's piece, as in the aforementioned fascinations with Brooks and Hobart, is not so much that these once-obscure individuals are elevated to attention (although that does matter); it is rather the mode of attention that Tynan, Cornell, and McElhaney take toward the subject of their affection, the writing produced out of their attentive way of looking at cinema, that is enduring. The performer is brought back to life in the fabric of writing.

Kinoshita's beautiful cinema, with which I began this section, is itself an elegant tapestry. *The Girl I Loved* captures and then provides a rhythmic context for Kuniko Igawa's performance, something of an equivalent to the writing (and, in Cornell's case, the film collage) I've discussed hitherto. Kuniko Igawa was not a big star in Japan and was far from the top of Shochiku's star roster at the time she made *The Girl I Loved* for Kinoshita. And *The Girl I Loved* is not the best remembered of Kinoshita's films; his later narratives that are more firmly rooted in Japanese history (*The Ballad of Narayama*, 1958) or sociology (*Twenty-Four Eyes*, 1954) have received more critical attention. Igawa's performance and the way Kinoshita observes it are ultimately far more memorable than the rather thin romantic narrative structuring *The Girl I Loved*. The scene which I described at the outset of this section also weaves together gesture and movement in a blend of male and female ways of moving through the world, together with a memory of movement reincarnated. Jirô plays his harmonica and Yoshiko applies her feminine accoutrements, all while the dress of her dead mother dances in the wind. It is as if the song of the harmonica and Igawa's gestures work together to bring a departed body back to life, a dance of desire and memory that the film, for its part, assembles through a careful and sensitive montage.

A writerly love for film driven by performance might resist the idea of attempting to assemble these descriptions of performance into a "full" account of a whole—a whole film, a whole narrative, or even an entire scene, a fullness of experiential recovery which is, in any event, impossible. Instead, a writer moved by actors might write in a way driven by remembered moments from film performances. This is a way of moving across a larger collection of cinematic memories, of finding transitions and connections among remembered gestures, movements, and expressions that give shape and sense to a form of life spent watching films, which may include those performances not yet remembered by many other eyes. This distinguishes the present discussion of writing on performance from much of the work that is done in cinema studies on the historical trends of performance styles and from narratological accounts of how the brain processes information in perceiving the moving images which present the actors to us; it edges closer to creative writing, to sentences that value rather than fear the existentially ambiguous or generative "I."[32] Traditional accounts which avoid this personal inflection tell us little of our movement through the performances that become parts of our lives. I'd prefer to let these little moments of performance live on, in writing, as they are strung together alongside other moments, in an account of what was felt as one watched people live in films that held us for a little while.

Chapter 4

A HUMAN SOMETHING

Bernardo Bertolucci's *Luna* (1979) begins with a sequence attentive to intimate gestures. A child drips honey on its leg; a woman, played by Jill Clayburgh, kisses and sucks the honey off his flesh, and brings her lips, still licking the honey, up to his face. These frames are intimately situated alongside the bodies of the players—very close to a child with no capability for knowing he is being photographed here for a movie, and closer still to Clayburgh, who by contrast is aware of her status and capacity as a professional actor. Bertolucci's frame becomes engulfed by the intimacy shared here between two bodies, in the fiction a mother and child but in our initial perception of the images more immediate and physical (words defining the precise relationship between these two bodies are just slightly beyond our in-the-moment experience of their undulations). A cut away from this intimacy, briefly, as the camera pans across several objects—milk, coffee, a beach ball: there is a little world surrounding these two people—before returning to the mother's face, and from there panning to her honey-dipped finger, which guides itself into the son's mouth (Figure 4). A pause, a breath: Clayburgh looks down at the small child as he begins to cough, to choke a little on this honey, as the soundtrack is engulfed by her breath. Bertolucci's post-synch mixing has the effect, here, of raising Clayburgh's sighs and caring whispers to our attentive ears, as she becomes, momentarily, the lungs of the film itself. Eventually, she coaxes the baby's breathing back to normality. She then brings to his lips a glass of milk, which he rejects.

This bodily quivering in *Luna* is shared between two actors (one an adult possessed with self-awareness, the other a child who cannot be), and occurs prior to words, knowledge, and conceptual signification. The images are presented less as building blocks for a story event and more as inhalations and exhalations, life that breathes as the celluloid flows through the projector. This shared intimacy between mother and son, outside of language, and yet at the same time inscribed within it, is generated by Bertolucci's language, his way of arranging images. As the film proceeds, this son will grow up to be … but what words won't abstract his humanity, or rationalize the primal desires Bertolucci has inscribed in the opening sequence? They feel so present in the film's opening, these images and the people contained within them, but they become more distant, more absent, as words are grafted onto what this child becomes. Growth, and adulthood, Bertolucci seems to say, entail necessary abstractions, the growth of primal gestures and expressions into a social arrangement, a public performance, a legible identity, a story, and so on. So, let's say the boy grows up, in his teenage years, and becomes a junkie. (This is the blunt word his mother will use with angst later in the film, once she discovers his heroin addiction.) His great love for his mother, his need for her, will be accompanied by his paradoxical and repeated rejection of her. Were those initial images mere foreshadowing of that play between intimacy and rejection, a key motif in the drama to come? But they couldn't be. The child in this opening sequence is not a conscious performer. These are painfully direct gestures, unconscious. Our loving attention to them must eventually give way to story, to a break in intimacy.

Figure 4: *Luna* (1979).

Even after it is acknowledged that an analysis of performance might slow down a bit, and linger a little longer, as a film itself might linger on what an actor is doing, the question remains: what precisely does a film lover's obsession with movies bring to this account of the actor's work? To return to a question I posed earlier, is a particular love for or devotion to the cinema necessary for appreciation of performance? Isn't any viewer in search of a story able to see what Jill Clayburgh does alongside this child in Bertolucci's *Luna*, or to notice Bess Flowers (without necessarily being able to name her) lingering in the background of a Hollywood movie? Someone who loves watching performers do their work—someone who begins with the performer—does not particularly require the medium of film, and need not become a self-conscious connoisseur to fulfill a desire for that unforgettable gesture, an affecting smile, a striking movement. There is the stage of the traditional theater where one might watch actors, and a plethora of moving-image media, none of them particularly requiring cinematic obsession, offer opportunities for experiencing performance.

There is also the related fact that, as discussed earlier, many writers on the cinema have not taken actors as a priority when writing about film pleasure. Historically, cinephilia has anchored its love to the auteur, as James Morrison shows in his analysis of auteurism as a mode of discourse.[33] In thinking about the importance of the auteur in the pages of *Cahiers du cinéma* in the 1950s, Morrison reminds us that these French film lovers saw the film director as a potential source of artistry from within the bounds of the otherwise normative system of mainstream cinema, the "author" of a series of poetic, sensuous ruptures—not unlike the kinds of jolting sensations that Sergei Eisenstein theorized in his "montage of attractions" and that Tom Gunning describes, in his discussions of early cinema, as "the cinema of attractions." "Those sensations were the ones the auteurists sought most vitally," Morrison writes, "and in their work 'ideas' serve as the mechanism of transmission, the crucial vehicle for the transference of feeling from auteur to spectator *through* the text."[34] Curiously, this aesthetic communication of ideas and emotions from the auteur is an exchange between a thoroughly absent figure—the director orchestrating the movements and sounds on the screen—and the viewer, absent to the actors onscreen and invisible, sitting in the dark. "But much more than in the cases of movie stars or characters within the fiction," Morrison writes, "encounters with authors entail identifications with an absence [...] Authorial communication through fictive texts is indirect by definition, and the work of film directing happens always somewhere else, other than 'in' the text, even if signs of it can be traced."[35] Actors, of course, can take center stage intermittently in auteurism, figures whose particular onscreen placement at any given moment is one possible trace of the "authoring" by the auteur in question. In such a case, familiar actors become one of the ways in which the absent auteur becomes "present" to us.

By contrast, in loving the performer, a viewer must grapple with a different sort of absence: her own. Stanley Cavell, in his discussion of the difference between theater and cinema in *The World Viewed*, begins not with a fundamental difference between the two mediums: the fact that in the theater the flesh-and-blood actor stands atop the stage, while in cinema it is only the actor's reproduced image that flickers on the screen before us. Cavell does not begin with the actor, but rather with the viewer, and with the diverging ways the mediums of cinema and stage situate the viewer in two respective kinds of audience:

> The audience in a theater can be defined as those to whom the actors are present while they are not present to the actors. But movies allow the audience to be mechanically absent. The fact that I am invisible and inaudible to the actors, and fixed in position, no longer needs accounting for ... In viewing a movie my helplessness is mechanically assured: I am present not at something happening, which I must confirm, but at something that has happened, which I absorb (like a memory).[36]

Cavell is beginning with his own viewing self, the "I" he discovers himself to be during films, a writer whose words signal for us an audience we might wish to join, or which we now recognize, as we read Cavell, being already a part of. And being a viewer in the audience at the cinema, for Cavell, renders absence as fundamental to the viewer's relationship to the actor. This is different from being a member of an audience at a stage play. The viewer of a stage play remains absent from the actor so long as social conventions are dutifully followed: in theater, the passions roused by the enacted drama presumably do not provoke us to rush the stage and become involved in the drama ourselves. We remain in the theater comfortably separate from the actor's shaping of onstage reality. In the medium of cinema, the viewer is not usually so conscious of a need to uphold social conventions of attending a performance. The film viewer's absence to the projected image of the actor is, in Cavell's phrase, "mechanically assured" by the apparatus of cinema itself, whether it be the projector in the movie theater or a screen at home; anyone so enchanted by, so taken with, a performer in a movie so as to rush the screen becomes the yokel in Jean-Luc Godard's *Les Carabiniers* (1963) who so craves a cinematically projected human figure that he crashes through the screen in a bid to fulfill his desire. Yet the figure to whom we are initially absent in cinema is not finally only a mechanical ghost; it is a viewer's attention, her way of seeing that actor—her "I" in dialogue with the absent "I" as expressed by the performer viewed—which gives that figure, and the viewer's own "I," her way of seeing, a lively kind of life that takes on palpable and singular presence in an event of viewing. For Cavell—as he goes on to write, after the passage quoted above—the actor in cinema only becomes a "human something," something more than only a recording of life past, when our eyes bestow attention upon her. Once our eyes dart to the actor on the screen—an attention solicited, no doubt, by the darts the actor has thrown at us—absence becomes presence. The viewer's way of seeing now both incarnates an actor (who has through a creative way of inhabiting the cinema screen perhaps made the viewer aware of the incipient creativity of her own way of seeing) and at the very same time confirms the viewer's own passionate embodiment, her presence alongside (even if still not *to*) the performer. Cavell: we are "present *at* him, *because looking at him*, but not present *to* him."[37] It is a memory of the past, become incarnate, made something human, something like flesh, through the loving attention of our eyes.

The idea that viewers might become so taken with a human being recorded and projected through the medium of movies that we forget—for a moment, or for a string of several moments—that what we are looking at is not a flesh-and-blood human being at all but rather a series of rapidly flickering representations of one who once stood in front of the camera, is a momentary forgetting of our own absence to the actors we see on the screen. We seem present and alive in our viewing precisely because a "human something" is now perceived as present and alive before us. We do seem present *to* the actor in these moments, even most vulnerably so, and this is a productive illusion. In these moments of realization, the actor's performance (regardless of the actual shot distance used by the filmmaker) becomes a close-up in our mind's eye, cherished there and held delicately in memory as a film flows on.[38] But it's the very intensity of this fleeting attachment that also threatens to block thinking through this experience. When our eyes "connect" to an actor on the screen, an occasional first tendency (this is not Cavell's tendency, but it might be ours) is to leap to psychological identification or abstract, narrative motivation—that is, "filling in" with meaning the time we spent with her. The character is thinking *this*, so she must be wanting to do *that*, and so on and down the causality chain. This is what haunts my description of the opening sequence of *Luna*: if all that intense, gestural presence is merely a narrative building-block, then perhaps presence is always fated to become absence, to become engulfed by the abstractions of narrative and meaning. This tendency obscures that unique incarnation, that mode of presence, of both viewer and actor that the viewer found through her eyes. What is onscreen is not at any instance a fully formed character but rather always-already fragmented gestures and expressions, pieces of a larger fabric knitted together not through abstract concepts but rather through the whole glimpsed in a mind's eye, a whole finally formed by a loving attention. That attention manifests itself a little differently for each of us but in ways that are nevertheless sufficiently similar enough to sensibly share.

In a love for cinema marked by the name of the auteur, it is the auteur's very absence from the events onscreen that orchestrates critical thought.

The desire for an author animates our writing. I say "Bertolucci's *Luna,*" yet Bertolucci is physically absent from the object he would seem to so possess—the film he has created. In loving performers, one finds oneself initially absent from, and yet desiring, the world of humanity created by actors onscreen. But in lightning-quick moments of fascination, our living presence at the film is confirmed and, in turn, the actor's presence is confirmed to us. These two forms of loving and living with the cinema, a love for actors and a love for auteurs, need not be mutually exclusive, although they do create tension: by itself, the phrase "Bertolucci's *Luna,*" as a linguistic marker that points to a film I might want to write about, ultimately makes absent the actors for whom, in my viewing, seemed so present and alive. More words must follow to make them present again.

Chapter 5

GESTURE AND DESIRE

Argentinian filmmaker Leonardo Favio's *Crónica de un niño solo* (*Chronicle of a Lonely Child*, 1965) poeticizes the experiences of young boys subject to the repressive conditions of reform schools on the outskirts of small, impoverished shantytowns. Favio's aesthetic blends influences from romantic varieties of European art cinema (particularly François Truffaut's *The 400 Blows*, to which the film explicitly refers) and a filmmaking approach sensitive to the interactions of the people in front of the camera. His actors in *Crónica* are mostly young boys, and when Favio's viewer first sees them it is in the reform school, an institution designed to keep desire under lock and key; the boys encounter long and seemingly endless corridors, in an architecture of steel bars and twisting staircases. In one scene, Favio's camera shows us several boys, scattered in a cavernous room that reverberates with the echoes of playing, yelling, crying. Most of these little gestures and expressions convey frustrated desire, stuck in a loop of repetitions: one boy cradles the head of another in his lap, as they pass the time; another spits again and again, onto the floor; two boys, in close-up on either side of the screen, blow a marble back and forth; another kicks a little ball against a wall.

One of these boys, holding before him a magazine page engulfed by Monica Vitti's visage, very cautiously glances for a few seconds across the room; his eyes nearly meet the camera directly, as if the very viewer of *Crónica* were policing his behavior, too. After a moment, he brings the Vitti photograph to his face; bending the pages of the magazines backwards, as if in imitation of the lover's caress of the head, he kisses the paper on which are reproduced Vitti's lips. A cut to a shot of some other boys leaves him in the middle of this kiss, as if suspended in private, confused ecstasy. Later in this montage, the film will return to this boy, who is now asleep (or feigning it), his head resting next to the photographic image of Vitti, the palm of his hand frozen in a caress of the magazine page (Figure 5). The earlier kiss and, here, the outstretched hand, begin in fantasy, but they end by implying something else: a desire to make the fantasy incarnate, to make the idealized image real and palpable, through gesture.

Figure 5: *Crónica de un niño solo* (*Chronicle of a Lonely Child*, 1965).

Writers such as Giorgio Agamben, Nicole Brenez, Adrian Martin, and D.N. Rodowick have used the concept of the figure, or the *figural*, to make manifest in the act of critical writing the material reality of the performer's work. For these writers, the figural element in a film is both a material part of the sensuous object that is any film—something we see onscreen—and the equally material and sensuous figuration that constitutes critical writing. The idea of figuration is key to the framework Lesley Stern and George Kouvaros provide in their 1999 collection of essays on performance, *Falling for You*. In their introduction, Stern and Kouvaros advocate for an approach driven by ekphrasis, a rhetoric that describes in writing some aspect of an art object. "In order to set the scene before the eyes of the reader," Stern and Kouvaros write, "the writer needs to deploy a notional ekphrasis, or a degree of fictionalisation. This is not to turn the film into a fiction; but in order to turn the film into writing, in order to convey movement, corporeal presence, performative modalities and affective inflections, a certain refiguring is required, an attentiveness to the fictional impulse at the heart of any ekphrastic endeavour."[39] The essays gathered together by Stern and Kouvaros do hover around the idea of performance, although more often than not this is tethered more broadly to the idea of "movement," in which anything flitting about onscreen might energize the descriptive powers of the ekphrastic critic.

In this sense, the very word "figural" signals an intention to write about more than, or other than, actors. In Nicole Brenez's study of Abel Ferrara, actors take on a figural function alongside other elements of Ferrara's cinema, and Brenez's criticism is itself a figural current running through the intellectual, sensual economy of Ferrara's films.[40] "Figural," as it is used in such work, implicitly accords with the terminology offered by David Bordwell, Kristin Thompson, and Jeff Smith in their introductory and widely utilized textbook *Film Art*, in which they remind us that a figure in a film is anything that moves—and since everything moves in cinema, at 24 frames per second, anything glimpsed in a film could be a figure. This conceptual breadth is both the strength and, relative to a concern for performance, the weakness of figural writing. These writers perform marvelous work in drawing our attention to a film's material, sensuous reality, weaving together a consideration of the presence of human figures in cinema with other manifestations and intensities. But at the very same time figural analysis also threatens to level out the actor with all other moving things in a film, which for a lover of performance has the effect of blunting and obscuring gestures, expressions, and movements—Garbo's face, Hayakawa's torso, Chaplin's eyes—alive in moviegoing memories. Joseph Cornell, in his homage to Rose Hobart, clearly would not stand for such a thing: if Hobart becomes a fascinating figure for him in his found-footage resurrection of her movements, it is undeniable that Hobart, as viewed on a cinema screen, is always the central player in the figuration. Figural analysis, by contrast, threatens to turn the actor into a bit player. In this form of writing, the paintbrush with which Kirk Douglas, playing Van Gogh, paints, in Vincente Minnelli's *Lust for Life* (1956), is a moving figure potentially equal to Douglas himself. The performer, and especially the movie star, is cut down to size with this method, no more a priority than any other prop that might strike one's fancy.

Figural writing, for all that it does in liberating the analyst to enjoy a free and creative play of material signifiers, in which the writer's writing becomes itself a kind of productive figure, threatens to repress something else about movie stars, that very something the boy in *Crónica de un niño solo* is careful to hide away from the judgmental glances of his peers: the sheer, swooning infatuation with the performer, the fact that, at least for a moment, other onscreen figures do not matter so much when a beloved is on the screen. As a filmmaker, Favio, in *Crónica*, is tapping into something that is almost embarrassingly familiar, a rote cliché that is the origin even of the present text: a childish infatuation with an adult movie star, with all the mystery of the future and of sex that, in young people, is variously disciplined and repressed. Yet Favio, the filmmaker, does not treat these two little gestures his young actor creates for his character—the kiss on the Vitti-image's lips, or the hand he places by her visage as, later, he sleeps next to it—with condescending scorn. Nor are they only woven into his écriture as a filmmaker: he lets these little moments with the boy and Vitti linger; they have their own kind of autonomous energy, remaining mostly unconnected to the larger story. In fact, for a moment, a viewer is given enough time to arrive at the impression that the boy, for his part, likely also feels: that through this kiss or outstretched hand he might make his fantasy incarnate, might make the glamour shot of Vitti come alive, through the movement and gesturing of his own body.

To approach an onscreen figure in this way (and here I turn from the boy's fixation on the frozen image of Vitti to an adult's fascination with moving figures in the multiple frames that make up a film)—as a figure not "traced" alongside others but a figure isolated and desired, something felt to be alive during viewing—is reminiscent of the presence Stanley Cavell talks about when he writes about experiencing the work of an actor in movies. But it also indicates the curious relationship that exists between the lover of performance and the reality on the screen, between the besotted viewer and what film theorists call the *indexical* aspect of photographic cinema. I admit that to cite a concept like the "indexical"—especially when placed in those scare quotes!—threatens to swerve creative writing on film performance into the byways of theory—that is, into an illustration of concepts that exist prior to and in excess of the actor herself. But it's a risk worth taking, because I think this and related concepts can live alongside performance in a creative way. "Indexicality" has been a key idea in film studies, and particularly in the short-lived cinephilic turn in the discipline (which was not always theoretical in nature). The *indexical* refers to the materiality of photographic-based cinema, that vivid reality which shimmers on the screen: the performed reality that is orchestrated before the camera at the moment of filming, a moment during which lively contingencies also hover before the camera's otherwise impassive mechanical gaze, such as the improvised movement of an actor, or the wind blowing in the trees. Christian Keathley discusses this idea via André Bazin's writings. Keathley writes that it is the "sensuous, material quality of film that Bazin was so fascinated with, and he regularly celebrated—indeed, fetishized—those filmic moments in which such materiality erupted with great force."[41] Keathley also links it to Roland Barthes' idea of the *punctum*, an element glimpsed in a photograph (or in a film) that strikes deep, piercing emotional guardedness in ways that go beyond the "dominant" forms of reading and interpreting the cinema (reading for story, seeking identification with character). The *indexical*, as a quality of (photographic-based) cinema, works somewhat in contrast to what theorists call the *iconic* properties of film images—images that seem to point to certain meanings without necessarily embodying them, in the way that a weathervane points to the idea of wind without precisely incarnating it—and *symbolic* properties, the abstract interpretations, for example, assigned to films, which are produced out of chains of images taken to satisfy the respectable academic's fetish for important, meaningful, and metaphorically transformative signification.

The place of the performer in such theoretical discussions of photographic-based cinema would seem clear: the actor is part of the indexical world that stands before the camera, part of the reality the camera captures as it records onto film traces of reality arranged and placed before it. In *A Bill of Divorcement*, both Katharine Hepburn and the staircase on which she walks are indexical traces; they were both really there, in front of the camera, registered by its lens and captured for our viewing. The ways in which writers on film often fall back on describing performance would seem to indicate that the performer becomes a kind of indexical trace, a figure; the gesture of the hand is inscribed onto film like the blowing of the wind through the trees. Jean-Luc Godard, for example, describing a moment from a film, uses language that implicitly reinforces this idea that cinema captures performance as part of its recording of reality: "In *The Magnificent Ambersons*, it is not the famous kitchen scene which I find shattering but, in this atmosphere of the twilight of the gods, the little face clutching at happiness which Welles has secured from Anne Baxter."[42] As Keathley notes, Godard here seems "to be referring [to] a close-up of Baxter's character, Lucy Morgan, her hat perched awkwardly atop her head, after she has bid a sad farewell to her true love, George Minafer (Tim Holt)."[43] As such, it certainly qualifies as something salient in Godard's singular experience of the film, a little fragment from the slice of filmed reality that has caught his eye. And yet what is ultimately more important to Godard is Welles's *seizing* of Baxter's visage via the camera (which enables Godard to seize in his writing the performance, and the film), the ability to incorporate her visage into the film's flow. What Baxter is doing is less the source of his fascination—and this is evident in the fact that Godard has not actually described her performance in this quote—than the camera's ability to capture her expression as a part of the mise en scène arranged and placed before it.

The point is not really that Godard should have described what Baxter was doing a bit more, although he could have. Rather, the larger point is that once a writer begins to pay attention to the work of actors, and to describe the work of performance in some detail, she unavoidably slips slightly beyond the indexical register, incorporating elements of both the iconic and the symbolic alongside descriptions of the immediately sensuous reality of a film. Actors, after all, are obviously not only indexical traces placed before a camera; they are something slightly *other* than the wind in the trees. A camera which captures the movement of leaves rustling through a tree is bearing witness to a moment of natural contingency, a figuration emerging naturally from a surrounding environment. Those trees would blow in the wind even if the camera hadn't been there. But actors, who know very well about the presence of the camera, train diligently to reduce contingencies, or what most professional actors would simply call accidents. Acting is a product of training, often of a system, which is dependent on strategies that vary according to the narrative situation to be enacted, the historical moment of production, and the interpersonal, creative context that forms the making of a particular film.[44] Actors do not simply let themselves be seized by a camera; they are also performing for it—in moments of virtuosity, they might be seen to seize it themselves. And at the same time, many star actors are also *icons*: in their way, they function not unlike a weathervane which gestures toward a wind it can only indicate. As P. David Marshall writes, a film star potentially becomes iconic when "what the icon represents is the possibility that the celebrity has actually entered the language of the culture and can exist whether the celebrity continues to 'perform' or dies."[45] Jonathan Goldman suggests that an icon is a screen figure that, like the weathervane, "points" to certain shared cultural or social meanings an audience will recognize. As he writes, "celebrity images, specifically, those legitimated by audiences that grasp their meaning instantly […] act as transcendent signs of their times."[46] Such a film performer bears the traces of cultural meanings and values that are symbolized, or made legible, in their image: Marlon Brando, Marilyn Monroe, and Charlie Chaplin are all examples of performers whose cultural significance arguably transcends, even as it emerges from, particular instances of film performance.

Actors, especially well-known actors, are in this way always potentially more—and less—than the presence they create on film: they carry aspects of the symbolic—they contribute to the meaning of a film, and to its narrative; and they are potentially iconic—they point to cultural and historical meanings surrounding the performance. The fact that actors potentially have symbolic and iconic properties in addition to sheerly indexical ones does not necessarily reduce the importance of the physical imprint they leave on film; a love for performance should not give up its fascination with that imprint, and with where it might lead, regardless of whatever preexisting discursive baggage attaches itself to the performance. The fact that some performers carry all three of these qualities with them can even make their indexical qualities—their qualities of inhabiting our lives in personal and unpredictable ways—especially striking. In *Crónica du un niño solo*, a young boy gestures toward a photograph of Monica Vitti. There, she is something other than a trace: she is an icon, a glamorous star, a visage which points to a larger cultural fascination, in the same culture in which this young boy is growing up. But this boy, as his hand gestures toward Vitti's face in near sleep, is not contemplating those iconic and symbolic registers. His gesture toward the icon, and the symbol, of Vitti in this photograph is implicitly a desire to touch something real and generative, not encumbered by already-articulated social and cultural predeterminations of response. In a desire for the performer, the viewer's gesture toward the actor—and the adoring hand of the child on the cherished photograph of a film star is not so far in time from the hand used by the adult to write about an actor—is not simply witness to an index of a reality past, placed and choreographed in front a camera a long time ago. It is also a gesture toward the future, toward a writing in which the meaning of the performer might, rather than only reinforce things already known about cinema, playfully unsettle imaginations.

Chapter 6

BROKEN GLASS

Anna (Isabelle Adjani) is having an affair. Her husband, Mark (Sam Neill) has hired a private investigator (Carl Duering) to follow her. This is the outline of a very familiar narrative situation, but the cinematic proscenium created by Andrzej Żuławski's *Possession* (1981) cracks convention apart, freeing the film and the performances to thrive on edges and fissures. Isabelle Adjani's performance dances on Żuławski's aesthetic as if it were broken glass, her characterization of a damaged, and damaging, woman jaggedly in tune with the filmmaker's discordant style. Żuławski catalyzes this dance between auteur and actor, his reputation as a filmmaker who brings his actors to the brink of physical and psychological exhaustion metaphorized in his cinema through the occasional tracking-forward of the camera toward the body of the performer, as if pressing against her. And this is how the confrontation between Anna and the investigator who has tracked her down to her hiding spot in a dilapidated apartment begins: as he enters, claiming he is there to check up on the windows, the camera tracks along to meet him at the door, eventually revealing Adjani on the right side of the frame, standing still against the side of the wall. A cut to a frontal shot of Adjani, the camera slowly and persistently pressing toward her face as she expresses wild-eyed, gaping fear. The camera in this scene is not quite assuming the detective's perspective; at two points during this moment, Żuławski will cut away from this frontal shot, which presses ever more intensely to an eventual close-up of Adjani's anguished expression, to a pair of shots, taken from different sides of the wall, in which the camera describes a half-circle around the pair as the detective moves closer to Adjani. Arranged this way, the cutting links the moving camera with the invasion of a private space, but only loosely, reminding us that the real dance here is not between Anna and the investigator, not even between Adjani and Duering, but between Adjani and the surrounding form of the film. The filmmaking choices generate a sense of a shattered world, one that can only be glimpsed through sudden changes in angle and unexpected framings, a world within which Adjani's Anna, ill-suited to the domesticity from which she has fled, can breathe and thrive.

And kill. This is, after all, a horror film. This private investigator won't make it out of this apartment alive. His pathetic demise punctuates the ascension of Adjani's moods and movements, which gradually transition from cowering tremors to dreadful, beguiling power. The detective begins "inspecting" the windows (but really looking for signs of the lover her husband suspects she keeps here), Żuławski's camera now following him as he moves over to a doorway within which Adjani is waiting. The moving camera parallels the exploration of space undertaken by the detective, but Adjani's performance repeatedly refuses to relinquish space to others, her sudden appearances in the frame, as the detective continues his work, pressing against his ostensible progress, and likewise bringing the camera to momentary stillness. Stopping the forward flow of pressing movement that had previously shaped the sequence, she now assumes a kind of mock-seductiveness, twirling the bandage on her neck as if it were luxurious fabric. The detective, resisting this mock-erotic temptation, slips to another window. The camera passes by Adjani to follow him but neither the camera nor the detective can avoid her quite so easily: before she is offscreen she emits a little expanse of breath, suggestive of the beginnings of a laugh, amusement now the dominant mood rather than fear. This sense of a movement toward absurd hilarity is amplified during Adjani's next sudden appearance before the tracking camera, laughing with what is now outright derision at the detective as he goes to check the bathroom window. The detective pursues a rational order of knowledge, but Adjani's Anna seeks disorder and disruption: shaking her finger at him as she walks into the kitchen, her convulsive laughter brings her to a bottle of wine—"Yes, wine!" she declares with ecstatic pleasure, and with a hint of surprise at her own demonic powers, a moment that forms an exclamation point to her movements in the sequence so far. The detective leaves the room, to find in the corridor the squelching, squeaking, monstrous creature, the demon who has made a cuckold of Sam Neill, hiding in this little house of horrors. Adjani stays behind in the kitchen, dropping the wine bottle, the sound of shattering glass coming from offscreen as the camera stays fixed on a close shot of Adjani surveying the wreckage. "Oh! Broke!", her removal of the noun from the verb in this sentence complementing a performance, and a film, built on fragmented images and shards of gestures, movements, and sounds that refuse to be stitched together again (Figure 6; the subtitle on the blu-ray oddly "corrects" Adjani's removal of "it" in her speech). She will, in a moment, take a shard of this glass, and use it to violently vanquish her scene partner, as the slimy, nonhuman lover looks on. Adjani's screams punctuate this sequence, her Anna finally terrified not by any external antagonist but by the discovery of her own sublime power.

Figure 6: *Possession* (1981).

In most films, and in particular classical cinema, the idea of gesture, as James Morrison writes, "constitutes a nonverbal means of communication with a language of its own, like the visual structures of cinema itself, providing a bridge between film actors' performances and film form."[47] The gestures of actors "speak" to us, in tandem with a filmmaker's cinematic language, the filmic "gestures" that constitute all the various, possible permutations of staging and filming. Performative gestures and directorial gestures, in this way, work together to generate a filmic context. Jean-Luc Godard imagined something like a shared gestural rhythm between actors and the auteurs who frame and film them, using the figure of a romantic couple to imagine how the shape and structure of a film might be generated in tandem with actors' performances:

> If direction is a look, montage is a heart-beat. To foresee is the characteristic of both: but what one seeks to foresee in space, the other seeks in time. Suppose you notice a young girl in the street who attracts you. You hesitate to follow her. A quarter of a second. How to convey this hesitation. *Mise en scène* will answer the question, "How shall I approach her?" But in order to render explicit the other question, "Am I going to love her?," you are forced to bestow importance on the quarter of a second during which the two questions are born […]. This example shows that talking of *mise en scène* automatically implies montage. When montage effects surpass those of *mise en scène* in efficacity, the beauty of the latter is doubled, the unforeseen unveiling secrets by its charm in an operation analogous to using unknown qualities in mathematics.[48]

Godard stages his own neurotically self-conscious variation of the well-known romantic comedy trope of the "meet-cute." Such orchestrations of movement within and across shots are broadly familiar from scores of cinematic romances, wherein an existentially anguished lover hesitates before moving toward a potential beloved in a particular way—"How shall I approach her?", a question that can usually be answered in cinema through the movement of the approach itself—that is, through a particular movement manifest by an actor. The second question, "Am I going to love her?", cannot be answered through performance alone, although a performer might very well characterize the quality taken by a particular brooding over the question; an answer to this question requires other actors, other framings, other gestures—in short, the forward movement of the whole film, and its ensuing formal and narrative developments. It is typical enough in cinema to move through these romantic developments via editing, but that is only one resource filmmakers use to move along to an answer to the second question. For Godard, screen performance substantially constitutes one part of that answer, the *how*: how might onscreen lovers move toward one another, how might they invest mise en scène with life, with the particular erotic energy they bring to the screen. In turn, découpage—the French word for the preplanned cutting and arrangement of shots in a film—parses out these gestures and movements across many shots and sequences, in effect creating that filmic bridge, noted by Morrison, between the actor's gestures and the form of the film itself. The gesture of an actor is joined with the gesture of the filmmaker, as in, say, a match-on-action cut in a Classical Hollywood film, in which the movement of an actor joins the end of one shot to the beginning of the next. Here, cut and gesture bind and make seamless the movement of the film as a whole. And it is upon this bridge that we journey toward the answer to Godard's second question, "Am I going to love her?": that question about the future of one's love which so many films answer in the affirmative.

This idea of film style as a kind of metaphorical bridging of performance to the larger form created by the filmmaker—between the performed reality in front of the camera and the work of the filmmaker with the camera and cutting—is not unique to Godard's critical writing. André Bazin also used a metaphor of mobility and a more expansive one than the construct postulated by Godard. Bazin's metaphor sees the movement across a bridge, or a series of steps, as a path to understanding how particular films generate relationships between the performed reality onscreen and the construction of the film by the filmmaker—a construction that is also perceptually created by us as we engage temporally and existentially with a film's images. Perhaps the crucial difference between Godard's and Bazin's metaphor is that while Godard's is aimed toward understanding the performance of love onscreen, Bazin's sees the viewer as a performer, creatively moving from step to step, or stone to stone, in a singular working-through of a given film's gestures. In writing on Roberto Rossellini's *Paisan* (1946), Bazin, like Godard, is fascinated with the viewer's emotional experience of film form, and with the relationship between that form and the human reality performed in front of the camera. Unlike Godard in the example above, however, Bazin seeks to move an understanding of the bridge between gesture and film form beyond a romantic couple. In writing on the complex and often highly elliptical arrangement of action in Rossellini's cinema, Bazin writes:

> In any case, the filmmaker does not ordinarily show us everything. That is impossible—but the things he selects and the things he leaves out tend to form a logical pattern by way of which the mind passes easily from cause to effect. The technique of Rossellini undoubtedly maintains an intelligible succession of events, but these do not mesh like a chain with the sprockets of a wheel. The mind has to leap from one event to the other as one leaps from stone to stone in crossing a river. It may happen that one's foot hesitates between two rocks, or that one misses one's footing and slips. The mind does likewise. Actually, it is not of the essence of a stone to allow people to cross rivers without wetting their feet any more than the divisions of a melon exist to allow the head of the family to divide it equally. Facts are facts, our imagination makes use of them, but they do not exist inherently for this purpose.[49]

To reframe Bazin's ideas in terms of performance: In alighting upon a gesture—in a moment of performance by an actor who moves us—we are, in contradistinction to all the cinema which seems to exist to satisfy emotional longings, given no guarantee of smooth movement to the next moment. We perhaps expect the perceived gesture to act as a kind of glue, a bridge, to our emotional and intellectual understanding of the entire film. As Godard reminds us, much cinema intends to generate precisely those kinds of emotionally satisfying experiences. But Bazin's example reminds us that in certain films we might miss our footing and slip (the act of watching a film is never a predetermined performance), as one emotion juts against a successive one that seems neither to answer nor confirm it, but perhaps acts in counterpoint or in dissolution of it. A bridge exists to make a connection, because it has been built that way. Classical cinema has been built—or has been seen as being built—to connect, to glue together, gesture and form. (Undoing this glue is part of what Joseph Cornell was doing in *Rose Hobart*.) This does not necessarily determine our emotional experience of classical works nor of the actors in them, but it does enable the possibility of satisfaction (the shape that satisfaction takes manifest in our accounts of the performances we love).

But actors and their gestures do not exist inherently to satisfy emotional longings, nor do they promise complete and satisfying identification. We might use stones to cross a river, momentarily taking them as a bridge, paralleling how we might see in actors some reflection of ourselves. But the emotional experiences and lives of the characters they create finally slip away from us. Encountering performance is frequently an encounter with difference and separation, at least as much as it is an experience of intersubjectivity. And when actors and filmmakers work to tap into this sublimity, the cinema they create together can often shatter, rather than build, sensual identification.

The cinema of Andrzej Żuławski is a cinema of shattering. There can be no doubt about the intense connection possible between the viewing eye and the performative body in his cinema; his are deliriously erotic and sensually engrossing films. But unlike Godard's description of a classical meet-cute, the questions and uncertainties felt within performance in Żuławski's films are never carefully joined or bridged to a form that arranges emotional relationships to the performer in a logical or expected manner. The pressure Żuławski places on performers in his work suggests he is not simply using them as one element among many to be arranged and ordered in his cinema, but as the most salient element. In Żuławski, gesture does not bind with cutting to create cinema; gesture, in his films, *is* cinema.

This can be seen in Żuławski's nearly complete rejection, in *Possession*, of the smooth match-on-action orchestration of performance familiar from classical cinema. It is not simply that his is a modernist cinema of discontinuous cuts, of the kind Godard uses in *A bout de souffle* (1960), for example. In fact, Żuławski's films often do have a kind of flow, and the images do not always function with the kinds of jump-cuts that animate some forms of modernist cinema. His rejection of seamless match-on-action comes not through recourse to an alternative ideology of image arrangement, but rather through a different orchestration of performance. Part of what makes *Possession*, and Isabelle Adjani's performance in it, so compelling, is precisely that these distinctions between a formal property of the film itself (a cut, a camera movement, a framing), put there by the filmmaker, and a gesture or movement by the actor herself, become utterly collapsed. If Żuławski and Adjani are here destroying the conventional form of cinema, they are doing so together. The jarring gestures and expressions by an actor in a Żuławski film often greet the viewer immediately, at the very beginning of a shot, their angular, performative incursion matching the incursion of the splice itself. But this is not a classical "match" that seamlessly hides the splice behind the gesture in its binding of cause-and-effect, action-with-continued-action, gesture-and-shot. Instead, gestures and cuts in Żuławski tear the fabric of existing connections, undo seams. They work together to disrupt, unbind, unsettle, rendering individual images little gestural islands, calling into question rather than enabling the possibility of connection, succession, order.

Chapter 7

A WAY OF MOVING

A performer's gestures, in all kinds of films, can also appear as part of a hidden web: they can hint at a secret coherence awaiting intuitive discovery, other ways of seeing a film.

Charles Burnett's *My Brother's Wedding* (1983) sprawls across the urban and residential areas of Watts, a predominantly African American community near Los Angeles. Pierce Mundy, the film's central character, is played by Everette Silas. We know Mundy only as Silas expresses him, through voice, body, and glance, which is to say, as a flighty being one minute—a man given to running, slipping away—and a hesitant one the next—equally adept at standing still, warily glancing at others who orbit the edges of his world. He is committed to his family but at the same time only dutifully present at work (he is employed by his parents), and always likely to drift into dalliance with Solider (Ronald E. Bell), a childhood friend. Silas—a lanky, spindly performer, tall and fragile in equal measure—expresses Mundy's tentative commitment to his environment through concrete gestures: his hands are the dominant motif of his performance, and they hold objects even as his legs at times urge him away (the final shot of the film, in which he holds the rings for his brother's wedding, is emblematic of Silas's expressive use of his hands). Silas's gestures toward people are primarily those of embracement, and of care, frequently taking the form of a hand or an arm around another's shoulder. Such gestures are performed by Silas early in the film, when Pierce visits Mrs. Richards (Sally Easter), the mother of Soldier, who is about to be released from prison. Burnett frames the beginning of this moment between Silas and Easter in a long shot, taken from the interior of a kitchen that looks out onto the dining room where Easter sits alone (Silas has yet to enter), contemplating a broken teacup she cradles in her hands. Silas soon enters the frame from the left, wraps his left arm around Easter's shoulder and back, and gives her an affectionate kiss on the cheek. This gesture grounds Silas, so often seen running to and from various places elsewhere in the film, into momentary stillness; it settles him into the calm he needs to reassure his friend's mother, who sees in Pierce an admirable adult in contrast to her troubled son, that Soldier has changed his ways. As the conversation continues, and after Burnett switches to closer views of Silas and Easter across shot and reaction-shot volleys, we see that Silas now cradles the broken teacup in his own hands, occasionally looking down at its two fractured pieces as he reassures Mrs. Richards that he and his son are "pretty much alike" (Figure 7). Like this teacup, perhaps: two childhood friends whose relationship will not easily be pieced together again. Hands and object, fingers and teacup: this gesture with the cup has emerged gracefully out of Silas's tendency to express Pierce's care for others through his hands. The same care he has shown for his friend's mother is now channeled into his attention toward a broken object.

Silas will repeat similar gestures at various moments in the film. We next see Silas embrace another figure in the dry cleaning establishment operated by his parents: as he swiftly runs into the backroom of the shop (Pierce is late to work, so he is running again), Silas affectionately guides his left hand across the shoulder and back of Dennis Kemper, the actor playing Pierce's father, Mr. Mundy, hunched over his work at a sewing machine, positioned to silently accept this loving, everyday gesture. Burnett has framed this shot in a way similar to his introduction of the moment shared between Silas and Easter: again the camera is positioned from inside one room as it looks out onto another, and again the actors are framed from a slight distance, giving us room to take in their shifting positions. But we are a little closer to Silas and Kemper here than we were to Silas and Easter in the earlier scene, and quite a bit closer to Jessie Holmes, playing Pierce's mother, Mrs. Mundy, who emerges from the backroom, after Pierce passes his father and begins to sort through some spools of thread hanging on the walls. Just as with the broken teacup in the earlier scene, Silas again directs his attention toward an object associated with one of his elders. Silas's gesture of embracement toward Kemper comically parallels and contrasts with the gesture Holmes greets him with as she passes through the room, as Mrs. Mundy pointedly admonishes her son—not with words, but with a much quicker and far less affectionate slap to his shoulder (tough love, in this case). Despite his running to and from commitments and responsibilities in this film, and for all of the loving attention he shows toward his elders and the objects that concern them, Pierce always seems a beat or two too late for them. His place in their world is confirmed not through narrative beats but is rather manifest in Silas's rhyming repetition of his character's everyday gestures of belonging and care.

Figure 7: *My Brother's Wedding* (1983).

These everyday gestures in *My Brother's Wedding*—the reaching of a hand toward a shoulder, or the careful consideration of a broken teacup or a spool of thread—are among the most interesting in cinema, precisely because they are not the most salient. It takes some work to detect them, because we do not typically perceive them, initially, as especially unusual: embracing another, and regretting broken objects, are a part of many forms of human life. But noticing these little bits of performative business in a film—and then remembering them, collecting them, and then arranging them in writing— is constitutive of a loving attention toward film performance, the desire to make a fragment part of a whole again.

In this respect, a love for performance expressed in writing, attuned to these fleeting gestures and movements, accords with the kind of attention to cinema practiced by V.F. Perkins. In his 1981 essay on Nicholas Ray's *In a Lonely Place*, Perkins writes about a series of subtle gestures he glimpses in the film:

> Suppose that you were planning the first few minutes of a film whose central issue is to be the uncertainty of emotion, a story of passion dogged by mistrust in which only the strength of feeling (not its nature) remains constant. You want to establish that neither hero nor heroine is sure whether the man's embrace is protective and loving or threatening, murderous [...]

That was Ray's problem at the start of *In a Lonely Place* (1950). His answer was to give the same gesture to three different characters within the brief space of the scene that establishes the film's Hollywood setting: each of them approaches another character from behind and grasps his shoulders with both hands. The first time, it is a perfunctory and patronizing greeting whose pretense of warmth is a bare cover for the assertion of superiority. Then, between the hero and an old friend, it conveys intimacy and genuine regard. Finally, when a large-mouthed producer uses the shoulders of the hero himself as a rostrum from which to publicize his latest triumph, it is seen as oppressive and openly slighting. These moments are significant in their own right, but their deeper purpose is—in a perfectly ordinary context—to dramatise the ambiguity of gesture itself.[50]

Andrew Klevan, writing of this passage, sees Perkins's words as a privileged example of how ambiguity and uncertainty are at play in specific moments in films, and in moments of writing about films. "The 'ambiguity of gesture'," Klevan writes, "occurs because the first and third gestures are both greetings *and* something else, and because all three taken together show how a similar category of gesture, customary and apparently insignificant, can take on a range of meanings."[51] Most of what I have written so far has focused on the emotional, memorial, or erotic dimensions of performance, but my example above from *My Brother's Wedding*—and, I think, Perkins's example from *In a Lonely Place*—are examples of something altogether more routine, grounded in an everyday life in which little gestures of affection can escape a viewer's attention precisely because they are so familiar. Such gestures are easily leapt over and missed by many viewers because they avoid the kind of spectacle and melodrama—and in the case of *My Brother's Wedding*, the compulsion toward romantic narrative—so often expected in film performance, particularly in Hollywood films.

Klevan, elsewhere in his work, has prized precisely these kinds of everyday gestures—he calls them "undramatic achievements": "When a human being is filmed, the performer encourages a process of comprehending their character which is full of indirections. Through watching their gestures, facial movements, movement in space, or the intonation of their voice, the viewers embark on a process of coming to *understand* character that is similar to that which they use in understanding people in the world around them."[52] This process of understanding characters while watching cinema arises through our careful attention to subtle movements and expressions by a performer across the body of the film, gestures that are easy to miss. The expressions of care or solidarity performed by Everette Silas—in his only documented screen appearance—in *My Brother's Wedding* and by Humphrey Bogart and others in *In a Lonely Place* are emblematic of gestures that often escape notice. They are also somewhat different than Barthes's fixation on Garbo's face or Epstein's fascination with Hayakawa's torso: these are not gestures that hold us in quite that way—particularly in the case of *My Brother's Wedding*, in which we are watching mostly nonprofessional actors in an independent film. It is nevertheless true that the narrative of *My Brother's Wedding*, as James Naremore notes in his study of Charles Burnett's films, contains occasionally jarring tonal shifts from the serious to the comic. A dinner scene in the second half of the film, in which Pierce encounters his soon-to-be sister-in-law (a haughty woman he finds distasteful), is marked by a kind of detached, nearly Brechtian style of performance completely bereft of the affectionate gestures I have pointed out in my description of other moments from the film.[53] But these arcane swerves in the film have their own connection to the everyday, for the quotidian worlds in which we live are occasionally marked by their own odd, unexpected shifts—the difference between one's behavior during a quiet Sunday morning, for example, and the way one performs at a social function such as a wedding or a business meeting, varying performances of "everyday life" examined by Erving Goffman in his classic study.[54] The everyday and the melodramatic—the easily missed gestures alongside more theatrical, ostensive, and declarative modes of being—often coinhabit the same film, sometimes within the same scene or performance.

The idea is not simply to note these machinations or contexts, but rather to live with them: to find a way of moving with the performer across the various gestural rapports that correspond to one another across a single film, or that speak across an actor's body of work, or in relationships discerned between different moments of performance collected in a life of viewing. If a filmmaker is resituating a performance, from one scene to the next, in the context of shifting tonalities, developing relationships, or evolving narrative situations, the viewer is also likewise adjusting across fluid and unstable emotional currents generated by the onward flow of a film, or of several films viewed in a passage of life. Sudden shifts in a performance's way of moving occur throughout *My Brother's Wedding*, but are harder to detect than, even as they are directly related to, the larger structural and tonal shifts of Burnett's handling of the narrative. Everette Silas is a performer who is present on the screen with everyday gestures and with a lanky, spindly gait that acts in counterpoint to the frequent stillness of Burnett's frame. I am reminded of a shot of Silas standing tall in the street, while talking to his friends, or relaxing during a night shift at the dry cleaners, his legs resting upward in the frame across the counter of the shop. These are moments of rest that are right for a character who seems, at least outwardly, happy enough where he is, who resists his parents' strident encouragements to move upward and onward with life even as he also demonstrates a settled kind of affection toward these older authority figures. So when we see Silas suddenly break out into running in the film—early on, during a sprint to his shift at the dry cleaners; or later, during a spree of innocuous troublemaking with Soldier, as he runs across the hilly sidewalks and curbs of the Watts neighborhood; or, most poignantly, in a sudden sprint across city streets after he is informed that his childhood friend has been killed—we move, too, from a restful, observational perception (resting alongside Silas as his character seeks to rest) to a nimble perception that readies itself for sudden changes and reassessments. These changes are generated by a performance that has shown itself capable of sudden bursts of movement, of shifts from lanky upright stillness to a sidewalk-leaping bound.

If an auteur-centered form of living with the cinema encourages a "way of looking"[55]—a way of seeing the mise en scène of a film—the love for film performance might be taken as a way of moving across that film, and in-between films: a way of forming gestural and expressive bonds between moments of performance and across the various moments of our lives in which we encounter them.

Chapter 8

A GLINT OF DEATHLESSNESS

I always felt that picture [*They All Laughed*] would never really work until everyone in the picture was dead, and then it would sort of become neutral again.

—Peter Bogdanovich[56]

The final third of this book looks at performances in two films directed by Peter Bogdanovich (1939–2022), *They All Laughed* (1981) and *The Thing Called Love* (1993). These films, I think, profitably resonate with many of the ideas about performance explored in the preceding pages.[57] Just like many of the other films and performers discussed in this book, *They All Laughed* and *The Thing Called Love* have become central to the time I have spent experiencing and thinking about performance in the cinema. And a relatively objective reason for looking at these two films in this book can be found in Bogdanovich's own history as a filmmaker, critic, and actor. As a director, Bogdanovich practices a filmmaking style more classically actor-driven than the comparatively baroque cinema created by his contemporaries who emerged during the moment of the Hollywood Renaissance in the 1970s. Those directors, all of whom deploy a more stylized approach to filmmaking than Bogdanovich, include Martin Scorsese, Brian De Palma, William Friedkin, and Robert Altman, the latter of whom, while in many respects an actor's director, does not employ a self-effacing style. Bogdanovich, more than his colleagues, is a classical filmmaker, whose style is energized by the presence of performers with whom his camera is frequently smitten. Bogdanovich, further, was himself a part-time actor, trained in his youth by Stella Adler and has appeared from time to time in his own films—see *Targets* (1968) and *Saint Jack* (1979)—and in screen work written and directed by others (most notably a seven-year supporting run as the therapist to Tony Soprano in the cable series *The Sopranos*). His understanding of acting as a director is in this way at least partially the product of having done a little bit of it himself. As a critic and historian, Bogdanovich, although known for his auteur studies of John Ford and Allan Dwan, also has a sharp interest in the art of acting. His 2005 volume of interviews with actors, *Who the Hell's In It*, is an important companion piece with his 1998 book of interviews with auteurs, *Who the Devil Made It*.

But there is another reason why I take these two Bogdanovich films as exemplars for a study of the love of performance. As earlier parts of this text have explored, a love for the performers who have lived for us in films finds itself haunted by absence. As I noted in the discussion of Stanley Cavell's reflections on performance, the actor is always absent to us in cinema, just as we are absent to the actor in our viewing; only through our response to performance do we and the actors onscreen take on life in an event of viewing. But even these treasured moments of performance become in their turn moments past, incarnated with performative breath and gesture before flickering away, like ghosts.[58] And it was always that way, even before we perceive that it is also, presently, that way for us. Dead movie stars are a given in older films, now that nearly all the performers from classical cinema have passed away. But death hovers around *They All Laughed* and *The Thing Called Love* in salient ways, and has since the years in which both films were initially released. Both films became associated with the untimely passing of their central stars: Dorothy Stratten, one of the stars of *They All Laughed* and Bogdanovich's lover at the time of the film's making, was murdered by her husband two weeks after the production of the film wrapped in the spring of 1980, and before editing on the film was complete; and River Phoenix, the young and rising star of *The Thing Called Love*, died of an accidental overdose outside the Viper Club in West Hollywood only three months after the theatrical release of the film in 1993.[59] When I became aware of these facts fairly early on in the time I spent with these two films (which was also fairly early in my own life), the foreclosed futures of Stratten and Phoenix became inextricable from, and eventually part of, the ways in which I experienced performances in each of the films.

Phoenix and Stratten are not the only performers in these two films whose presence enables loving writing on film. For many, it will undoubtedly be the presence of Audrey Hepburn in *They All Laughed*, in her last leading role in a major theatrical film prior to her own death in 1993, which resonates. The presence of Ben Gazzara (who passed away in 2012) in *They All Laughed*, a screen luminary known for his indelible work with the inimitable John Cassavetes, might also move some viewers. Indeed, the losses of Hepburn and Gazzara move me, too, and pierce my emotional experience of *They All Laughed* in their own way. But in ways that are particularly important for a discussion of Stratten and Phoenix, and as Bogdanovich himself points out in the quote at the beginning of this section, the distance of years that separate my writing from the initial appearances of these two films, and the tragic circumstances surrounding them, return *They All Laughed* and *The Thing Called Love* to something near a neutral position, enabling them to function again as lively experiences whose performers once again radiate, whenever the films are projected and if only for the time of that projection, with performative life. Nevertheless, the unfortunate deaths of both Stratten and Phoenix are also important to what I will ultimately frame here as the two films' celebration of performative life, a life that in this case is partially born out of loss and death.

As discussed earlier, indexicality, iconicity, and symbolism became key concepts in the short-lived cinephilic turn in film scholarship. In these two Bogdanovich films, however, the viewer encounters the unusual cases of two cinematic figures whose achievement of iconicity—their full establishment as film stars—was cut short by death. Death prevented Stratten and Phoenix from realizing their potential as performers—it prevented them from achieving iconic fullness.[60] There are other ways to phrase it, though, and more directly, without bothering with theory: one might convey the pang of the loss of these two talented and charming performers by writing that both Stratten and Phoenix were cut short at the height of their beauty, a beauty Bogdanovich, in each case, was well-positioned to capture on film. *They All Laughed*, edited in the wake of Stratten's death, could in part even be considered a hymn by Bogdanovich to Stratten's beauty. Regardless of the terms used, their deaths haunt the narratives of both films: the detective story that serves as the plot of *They All Laughed* involves a romantic triangle that uncannily evokes the real-life context that led to Stratten's murder; and the story of *The Thing Called Love*, which involves three young country singers aiming at stardom but which ends without confirming their success, resonates also with the loss of what more Phoenix might have achieved in films had he lived beyond the age of 33. Paradoxically, the fact that each actor's career was cut short by death, foreshortening their iconic fullness, enables both Stratten and Phoenix to remind us how the onscreen actor can exude a kind of indexical charge, even as performers undoubtedly also function as symbolic figures within a film's narrative form. Unlike the perceptual marginalia cinephiles often pride themselves on finding and curating, Stratten and Phoenix are in the center of the frame in these films, and are noticed, on some obvious level, by both casual moviegoers and more discerning film lovers. Their early deaths, and the incompleteness of their iconicity, make salient the ongoing charge they carry onscreen, the shots to the heart that, as I have suggested, actors can potentially fire at us and that can inspire a writer's effort to let performance live and breathe a little more on the page.

Chapter 9

POSSIBLE STARS

In *The Thing Called Love*, Samantha Mathis plays the main character, Miranda Presley. Mathis is the central focus in an ensemble of actors. Her Miranda is a New Yorker traveling to Nashville to write and sing country music. (Miranda's last name would seem to divine a successful career in country music, but as she tells other characters in the film, there is "no relation" to Elvis.) In the opening shots, Mathis nods away sleepily in a Greyhound bus that takes her from the big city to the American South. The film's opening montage is comprised of traveling shots of the New York City skyline—the city Miranda leaves—accompanied by country music, as Miranda is swiftly transported to The Bluebird Café in Nashville, where she will eke out a living as a waitress while writing her songs while also developing relationships with two country singers, played by Phoenix and Dermot Mulroney, who compete for her affections, and a friendship with another would-be singer, played by Sandra Bullock. The end of the narrative, as Miranda nearly gives up in her struggle to become a noted singer before returning to Nashville to try again, strikes a playfully ambiguous note. After Mathis gives a sterling performance of an original song called "God's a Woman," she leaves The Bluebird Café alongside both of her male paramours, and the film is as uncertain about which man she will choose, or if she *will* choose, as it is about whether any of the young singers in the film will achieve further success as artists or musicians.

There is one sequence in the film I always remember, and that I remember remembering with pleasure throughout the years in which I have spent time with this film; in the years before films were very soon available after release via digital download, and in which there was no available internet to look again and again at a trailer or a scene selected for publicity, I had to wait several months to see anything from the film again after I first saw it in a cinema during the summer of 1993. It is a moment of performative joy—the joy of gesture and music. Miranda is attending a country line-dance in Nashville. Singers croon songs on an outdoor stage while a large group of people gathered in front of the musicians line-dance to the music. Samantha Mathis tentatively steps and shimmies in rhythm with a song—still just freshly out of New York City, her Miranda waves her hands up and down while trying to figure out how to line-dance—as a backdrop of Nashvillians move more confidently and assuredly with this music (Figure 8). After a few seconds of conveying her character's failed attempts to adapt to this peculiarly country-fried form of bodily movement, Mathis, a luminous smile beaming across her face, quits her awkward country dance and starts jumping up and down while twirling in a circle, striking more of a rock-and-roll figure, a way of dancing that for this viewer is certainly more memorable and interesting than any correct education in country-music performance might be.

Figure 8: *The Thing Called Love* (1993).

Although my interest in *The Thing Called Love* lies mostly in its actors, their gestures and movements work in delightfully individualistic accord with Bogdanovich's own classical film style, which seems as interested in actors and their ways of moving as I am. In other words, this pleasure in *The Thing Called Love* inescapably joins the indexical—the sight of a performer on a particular night playing a character dancing in front of a particular camera—with the potentially iconic. My eyes, then and now, are glued to a performer, Samantha Mathis, with whom I was already familiar when I first went to see this film in 1993 (having no idea who Peter Bogdanovich was when I was 14 years old, I wanted to see the film not for him but for her). She was familiar to me from her roles in *Pump Up the Volume* (1990) and *This is My Life* (1992) and—I admit with a great deal less confidence in my teenaged-self's taste in movies—her role as the Princess in *Super Mario Bros.* (1993). By the time of its (very limited) release in theatres, I recall anticipating and desiring *The Thing Called Love* as a vehicle for Mathis as a possible star (no more or less well known at the time than *The Thing Called Love* costar Sandra Bullock, who would achieve the fame I imagined for Mathis the following year, in *Speed*). Mathis, although obviously already a successful actor in the film industry, nevertheless felt like a secret I was keeping to myself, a big movie star in the waiting. The stardom I imagined for Mathis didn't quite happen, a falling short of cultural iconicity that, as I'll later suggest, became important to my later, repeated viewings of this movie.

Although I was of course blissfully unaware of it while watching the movie for the first time three decades ago, tethering a desire for cinema to an appreciation of performance is a suitable response to engaging with Bogdanovich's actor-driven, classical cinema, which gives actors time and space to incarnate characters, and time for viewers to attend to details of performance. Gestures and movements such as the dancing and smiling of Samantha Mathis in *The Thing Called Love* become not disposable details on the way to an abstract notion of "character," but rather give us a palpable and unforgettable sense of the actor's presence onscreen; and they are not reducible to the "star gazing" of celebrity culture (even though, as I've admitted, my youthful interest in Mathis as a performer was tethered to my sense that others might see her the way I did—as a great movie star). Instead, our attention to particular choices made by an actor registered by the camera constitutes our very connection to the character and her place in the overall form of the film—the point at which a love for the indexical in cinema is joined to our pleasure in watching film icons (or potential icons—*possible* stars) on the screen.

And as I've suggested, Bogdanovich's films have always centered on appealing stars just as Bogdanovich's own cinephilia has been as appreciative of actors as it has been of auteurs. In his commentary track for the DVD release of *The Thing Called Love*, the director perceptively recounts his varying strategies in framing and cutting, in relation to the movements and positioning of the actors. At certain points in his commentary, he remarks upon his use of the long take, a stylistic approach utilizing traveling shots, to follow two or more actors over a relatively long duration, typically in scenes of conversation.[61] Such a choice underscores not only the indexical charge of the images (we are watching actors perform in ways that are relatively free of overt editorial intervention) but also indicates to the viewer moments in which the characters onscreen establish intersubjectivity with one another, and perhaps also with us—a temporary connection.

Editing does shape the performances in other respects, however. Throughout *The Thing Called Love*, when he wants to underscore the way a performance conveys the solitude of a character—in shots of Samantha Mathis as Miranda, working on her songs in the café, or organizing her things in her hotel room—Bogdanovich will rely on quicker cutting and closer framings, emphasizing isolation. In his long takes, by contrast, the director's classical style emphasizes how these performers, their characters struggling to achieve individual distinction in the Nashville music scene, are nevertheless able to form bonds and small groups based on the love they share (either personal or romantic love for one another, or a love for the music which brings them to Nashville). What is striking to me about the moment I described earlier—the moment in which Samantha Mathis dances—is that it involves both tendencies. It is a moment of togetherness, as the characters dance. But the relatively quicker cutting of the dancing scene, in tandem with Mathis's performance, also renders Mathis's subjectivity, her singular way of being in front of the camera, salient.

Chapter 10

A LITTLE LOVE

On my subsequent viewings of *The Thing Called Love* after first seeing it in a cinema upon its initial release, after the film became available on home video, I was aware that River Phoenix had died just a few months after the theatrical release of the film. I was unfamiliar with Phoenix's other performances; I was too young to have seen his celebrated work in *My Own Private Idaho* when it was released in 1991. *The Thing Called Love*, in this way, was both the beginning and the end of (at least during Phoenix's own life) my encounter with his performances. Where my initial viewing of the film in a theater fell under the spell of Mathis's radiance, my subsequent viewings on home video were my first self-conscious encounter with death in and around cinema, given my fresh attention to Phoenix's presence in the film as the character James Wright. On some level I had an awareness that the person onscreen, in a movie that was already very much part of my life, was now quite literally gone, his animation in the frames of a film no longer corresponding to any existing human outside of it. The absence of the actor, as described so beautifully by Cavell, was now ineluctable and permanent, an emotional attachment to a performer now tethered to a melancholy awareness of that performer's death.

My desire to see and perpetually re-see *The Thing Called Love* was born out of an attraction, which developed at different times and for different reasons, to two actors who did not quite become the stars they might have become—Phoenix, having died so heartbreakingly young, and Mathis, facing a future of mostly supporting roles in big movies and leading roles in small movies none of which, for me, were as enchanting as *The Thing Called Love*. Early death and the cutting short of stardom—of course not equivalent things, but in their way each a kind of loss—were also, as I discovered later, part of the context that accompanied the release of Peter Bogdanovich's earlier film, *They All Laughed*. Filmed in 1980 and released in 1981, *They All Laughed*, along with Michael Cimino's *Heaven's Gate* (1980), is often regarded as one of the last gasps of the New Hollywood era after the rise of the blockbuster film and before the emergence of the indie-film movement in the late eighties and early nineties. Entirely self-distributed by Bogdanovich after studio support for the film fell through, the postproduction and release of *They All Laughed* happened within the wake of Dorothy Stratten's tragic murder by her estranged husband shortly after the production of the film wrapped but before editing finished (a grisly turn of events later adapted on film, with the names changed, in Bob Fosse's 1983 film *Star 80*).[62] By the time I saw *They All Laughed*, I was aware of who Peter Bogdanovich was, having watched the film after having viewed nearly all of his other films in quick, retrospective succession, including my first viewing of *The Thing Called Love* in almost two decades. I was also aware that death, as it had cut short Stratten's nascent stardom in the early eighties, had by the time of my viewing taken the film's other major stars: Audrey Hepburn, alongside John Ritter (whom I had come to appreciate in another role for Bogdanovich, in *Nickelodeon*, as well as his hilarious, underrated performance for Blake Edwards in the 1989 film *Skin Deep*), and Ben Gazzara. Perhaps because of this, there was something about *They All Laughed* that reverberated for me, an intuition that the film had a secret correspondence with *The Thing Called Love*, the other Bogdanovich film around which also swirled the haunting specter of a performer's death. And the correspondence once again was about performative life in the cinema becoming incarnate—about experiencing love and forestalling death, living languorously in the moment even as it passes us by—through music and gesture.

They All Laughed centers on a group of private detectives spying on a somewhat smaller group of men and women—primarily women—who may or may not be having affairs. On first viewing, for nearly the first 40 minutes of *They All Laughed*, it is difficult, and not especially important, to ascertain exactly why Ben Gazzara's detective John Russo is trailing Audrey Hepburn's rather secretive Angela Niotes, with the assistance of a cab driver, played by Patti Hansen, named Deborah (whom John bequeaths, puzzlingly, with the name of Sam); or why John Ritter's detective Charles Rutledge and his pal played by Blaine Novak, Arthur Brodsky, are tailing Stratten's Dolores Martin, a woman with whom the shy Charles becomes very quickly smitten. Initially, as the first stretch of the film unfolds, it is even difficult to ascertain that these men are in fact private detectives—their way of following and looking, their way of watching, seems an entirely personal trait, rather than a fully institutionalized one. No doubt, this suggestion of a personal way of seeing resonates with how Bogdanovich himself approaches the making of the film. The John Ritter character is styled with large glasses to look something like Peter Bogdanovich circa 1980, giving his character's helpless infatuation with Dorothy Stratten, feelings Bogdanovich shared, a self-reflexive tinge. And Bogdanovich orchestrates the performances of all the actors in *They All Laughed* in a loose and playful way, as their eyelines playfully miss, slide by, and very occasionally match with one another as the film flows on. An infatuated way of looking, for Bogdanovich, is not a gaze, static and rigid, objectifying the figure of its affection. It is a way of living with a film and the people acting in it—for Bogdanovich, is a way of creating it—which in turn invites us to watch it playfully, in the spirit of the movement at play in the film. Midway through what is nominally the second act, nevertheless, the viewer of *They All Laughed* grasps something like a plot, as we finally learn that Ritter, Gazzara, and Novak are playing private detectives on the hunt for clues. Even after this plot motivation becomes clear, though, it is not the primary interest of the film, which continues to prioritize the secret emotions coursing through its performances: the way Gazzara, Hepburn, Ritter, and Stratten—along with Colleen Camp, playing a country singer named Christy Miller who is herself infatuated with, and voyeuristically trailing, John and Charles—circle around one another in a ring of desire, as Bogdanovich's camera and his cutting alternately connect and separate them.

Watching *They All Laughed* over 30 years after it was made, I remembered my youthful pleasure in the way *The Thing Called Love*, also a film haunted by the death of one of its stars, similarly animates gesture and music. *They All Laughed*, like the later Bogdanovich film, confirms the possible joys of life that might be depicted, or performed, in cinema, a sensibility which, in its open invitation to the viewer to share in the joy of watching and moving, generates intersubjectivity and connection, expressed again by Bogdanovich not only through his direction of actors but also in his editing rhythms and the way these create relationships between performers. Late in the film, the characters gather in a New York City club to hear Colleen Camp sing a few country songs. The gestures, movements, and eyelines at play in the performances are in this scene brought to a crescendo, resolving the film's intersecting relationships in the rhythmic way in which Bogdanovich stages and connects the various performers in and across the frame. His directing style not only enables loving attention to performance but also is itself a creative instance *of* that adoration for performers, as we watch a director, touched by death, nevertheless admiring and animating his players, at the moment of postproduction, in a tapestry of filmic life. We know now that a weary and devastated Bogdanovich, in the months after Stratten's death (which occurred after the film was shot but before it was assembled in the editing), was still cutting the film—arranging traces of performances into a potentially symbolic and iconic assemblage—making any close reading of gesture's relation to editing choices in *They All Laughed* retrospectively charged with melancholy life.

As Patti Hansen and Blaine Novak exchange words near the bar, John Ritter and Hansen glance at one another across the room, while Dorothy Stratten walks down the steps to meet Ritter at one of the tables. Surveying this roundabout of interaction is Colleen Camp, onstage: as she sings her songs she gestures and glances at several of the others, cueing each of them to recognize that others are there, or about to be there, and are perhaps still spying on one another. All of this is conveyed through Bogdanovich's rhythmic cutting, timed to gestures: Ritter removing his glasses to clear something from his eye (Figure 9); Camp gesturing with her hand to convey that she has received Hansen's message (Figure 10); Hansen moving her hand, in turn, to confirm that she has received Camp's implicit message; and so on. The rhythmic cutting of the editing joins these gestures and gazes and connects the performances with the progression of the song to create an especially memorable—and musical—sequence, an expression of how cinema, particularly cutting and rhythm, can share in, discover, and make manifest the music of gradually unfolding performative life.

Figure 9: *They All Laughed* (1981).

Figure 10: *They All Laughed* (1981).

That this gestural and musical expression of life is again expressed through movement to country music—this time in the guise of a singer, Camp's Christy Miller, who anticipates (and inverts) the journey of Samantha Mathis's Miranda in *The Thing Called Love*, having traveled from Nashville to New York City to live life as a country-singing city dweller—furthers my sense of a subterranean correspondence between the two films. Both films also begin with striking traveling shots of the New York City skyline, as accompanying country music plays over the opening credits and as the shots themselves accompany Camp and Mathis as each head in opposite directions. My accounts of these moments from both films, which move from an experience of solitary viewing—both the situation of film viewing and the solitary, individual presences at work within the films—to a cinematic orchestration of collectively experienced gestures and music, might be enough to suggest that *They All Laughed* and *The Thing Called Love*, despite the sad circumstances surrounding their release, offer a plenitude of ongoing, indexical pleasure, a generous offering of performative life. Such pleasure may even be oddly intensified, given the fact that at least two of their major stars, their lives and careers foreshortened by death, never achieved iconographical fullness in cinema.

There nevertheless is still something missing from this account of both films, something to do with this idea that films and the memorable performances within them remain elusive and sometimes incomplete, needing, like Jacques Rivette's regard for the films of Nicholas Ray, "a little love," a bit of compensatory affection. This love does not only balance out, or compensate for, the marginal positions *They All Laughed* and *The Thing Called Love* occupy in film culture and in accounts of Bogdanovich's work, but it also responds to the way love's gestures, in the performances themselves, compensate for loss and incompleteness.

Chapter 11

IN ANY OTHER PAIR OF EYES

Bogdanovich's own account of the postproduction of *They All Laughed* suggests that the film appeared in cinemas as something less than what he fully intended. In *The Killing of the Unicorn* (1984), his book about Dorothy Stratten's murder and the circumstances surrounding it, Bogdanovich starkly describes *They All Laughed* in the wake of Stratten's death. This writing becomes even more melancholy in relation to Bogdanovich's earlier writings on the cinema, which are more celebratory in their tone. "Then suddenly I remembered the movie Dorothy and I had made," Bogdanovich writes. "It had been killed as well, its two hours a moving photo album of our days together."[63] Bogdanovich's words suggest an ambiguous suspension of emotion in watching *They All Laughed* upon its completion in 1981, wherein its new status as a "moving photo album" upon Stratten's death pivots around two possible meanings of "moving": either as a film that might still possibly "move" a viewer emotionally, even after the tragedy surrounding its making; or in a more literal sense, in the idea that the film was now, in the wake of Stratten's death, little more than a "moving" collection of photos, unfolding one after the other, but no longer animated by joy. Writing these words so soon after Stratten's murder, and acknowledging in his sentence that the film had been for him "killed" by its sad circumstances, it is undoubtable that "moving" in Bogdanovich's intended meaning refers to the latter. But as time went on, Bogdanovich rediscovered something life-affirming in *They All Laughed*: in later interviews, the director will mention the film as his favorite of those he has made, and in one interview even refers to an especially personal version of the film, a private cut existing on a single 35 mm print only he possesses, and which is rarely screened for others.[64]

Bogdanovich's eventual rediscovery of his love for *They All Laughed* cues us to recognize the ongoingly incomplete status of the film, beyond the incompleteness of Stratten's sadly shortened career in cinema, in the sense that the auteur's own private affection for it remains separate from the film's continued public circulation on home video, and at occasional retrospective screenings, given that the director's own preferred version of the film is kept privately tucked away. These private emotions, however, have their own secret relationship to the later *The Thing Called Love* and its own status as an incomplete object. A director's cut of *The Thing Called Love*, distributed by Paramount on DVD in 2006, 13 years after the original release of the film, included approximately four additional minutes of footage. Many of these changes result in the extension of scenes involving the singing of songs, or small additional passages of dialogue. One extended scene enriches our understanding of Samantha Mathis's characterization of Miranda. Shortly after arriving in Nashville, Miranda checks into a small motel near The Bluebird Café. The joke is that the only room left is the "Village People Room," decorated with kitschy seventies popular culture comically distant from Miranda's passion for country music. The theatrical version of the film ends when Miranda enters this room and smirks at the interior decoration. In the director's cut, however, her entrance into the room lasts a bit longer. A held shot of Miranda's suitcase, after Mathis opens it, reveals several objects she has taken with her on her trip to New York City. Some of these are items that might belong to any lover of country music: cassettes of Elvis Presley and Johnny Cash. Around these, however, are other objects, including two books: *Collected Poems* and *The Greek Myths I*, by the English poet Robert Graves; and *A Room of One's Own*, by Virginia Woolf (Figure 11).

Figure 11: *The Thing Called Love* (1993).

As Bogdanovich's commentary track on the DVD suggests, the addition of these objects helps us get to know Miranda better as a character, and the Elvis Presley tape in particular refers to a later bit of dialogue between characters in the film.[65] But the books in her suitcase carry more subterranean resonances within Bogdanovich's own life, particularly as it developed after the filming of *They All Laughed*. Near the end of *The Killing of the Unicorn*, Bogdanovich mentions several literary works which helped him cope with Stratten's death, writings that prompted him to think more fully about the ways in which images of women circulate in American culture. (Stratten was exploited by *Playboy* magazine and Hugh Hefner comes under direct criticism in Bogdanovich's account of the events leading up to her murder.) The Graves and Woolf books, glimpsed in Miranda's suitcase in the director's cut of *The Thing Called Love*, are among the works he mentions. His account of their ideas takes the form of an anecdote:

> In the mid-seventies, Cybill Shepherd had read Graves's extraordinary "historical grammar of poetic myth," *The White Goddess*, along with his definitive collection of *The Greek Myths*, and one evening mentioned to me the essential premise of both books: that the earliest known civilizations had been matriarchal, that in the original "Beginning," Goddess, not God, had created Heaven and Earth. I remember laughing with a kind of cynical glee at the time: Having already learned by then that fame, success, money, and love were not as advertised by the established order, I didn't even find it particularly surprising that the accepted foundations of civilization were originally quite different too, and that God had once been called by a female name.[66]

Bogdanovich describes revisiting the Graves book after Stratten's death, leading to his reflections upon the circulation of images of women in Hollywood cinema, a discussion in which Bogdanovich cites a lengthy quote from Molly Haskell's landmark 1974 book *From Reverence to Rape*.[67] Bogdanovich's own grappling with these writings as he attempted to emotionally survive Stratten's death reemerges as a subterranean current in *The Thing Called Love* a decade later. What is particularly intriguing is Bogdanovich's bequeathing of his own connection to Graves's ideas and poetry to Samantha Mathis, and the character she is working to create, in the later film.

A little more than midway through *The Thing Called Love*, Mathis's Miranda and Phoenix's James begin to make love after returning from the line dance. They amble into the bedroom, Miranda gently but assertively pushing James onto the bed and climbing on top of him. The theatrical cut fades out shortly after this moment, but the director's cut of the film lingers

Figure 12: *The Thing Called Love* (1993).

a little longer with the two lovers.[68] Cutting to close shots of both characters as Miranda looms above James, the camera lies beneath Mathis (Figure 12) as she whispers these poetic lines—to Phoenix, and to us:

> *Assured by that same glint of deathlessness*
> *Which neither can surprise in any other pair of eyes*

These lines, from a poem called "Change," included in one of the Graves volumes glimpsed earlier in Miranda's suitcase and spoken here in the film's most significant love scene, are very likely words Bogdanovich encountered upon reading Graves's works after Stratten's death in the early eighties.[69] At no point in his DVD commentary track for *The Thing Called Love* does Bogdanovich mention the connection of these lines of poetry to the earlier film, or to his personal tragedy. Instead of claiming or possessing a public authorship over the inclusion of the poetry in his film on the commentary track—in the sense that so many commentary tracks do, as directors claim or seize what is seen and heard in the film as their authorized intention—Bogdanovich privately gifts this poetry to Samantha Mathis, whose utterance of the words is key to both the emotional and erotic tenor of the scene; and also, albeit indirectly, to River Phoenix, whose own early death would nevertheless be put into counterpoint with "that same glint of deathlessness" surrounding his beautiful eyes in *The Thing Called Love*. And perhaps he is also gifting these words to a viewer who might in turn be enchanted by both Mathis and Phoenix as they ongoingly live for us, whenever *The Thing Called Love* is projected.

This anecdotal account of performance in *The Thing Called Love* began with my recollecting a memory of Mathis's work, of her dancing pleasure as Miranda enjoys country music. My memory of this moment provided a phantom thread to my much later viewing of *They All Laughed*, which is itself about the joys of moving from individual points of glancing or looking to ways of movement, and ways of moving to points of joyful connection with others. Nevertheless, the marginal statuses of both films—in film culture generally, and in Bogdanovich's oeuvre particularly—remind us of the difficulty of moving from a private way of seeing performance to a collective sharing of that way of seeing, even as we watch performances that are themselves emblems of that very existential process. I have also underscored this point in my account of Bogdanovich's own personal relationship to *They All Laughed*, in both its public form and in his own private cut of the film, emotions which course through his later films, particularly *The Thing Called Love*, in hidden ways.

The poetic words Samantha Mathis speaks in the love scene described above also resonate, I think, with much of what I've tried to describe about the experience of film performance in these pages. Perhaps in watching her in *The Thing Called Love* when it was first released, I was not so different from the young boy caressing the image of Monica Vitti, encountered earlier in this book. As I watch Mathis whisper the lines from the Graves poem in the director's cut of the film today (with my awareness now that they are, in fact, lines from a poem), I wonder if I wanted to write my own words as a hymn to Mathis's beauty, somewhat as Bogdanovich did for Stratten in the shaping of his film. As an adult viewing this film now, Mathis invites a more complexly intersubjective encounter with her presence onscreen, her performance incarnating a subjectivity that is autonomous and vibrant and which now resonates within my knowledge of her director's larger body of work and with my interest in film performance generally. Mathis's reading of the poem—and Bogdanovich's gifting of it to her—reminds us how performance, and its directorial orchestration, can contribute unexpectedly and charmingly to a life with cinema. A way of seeing and a way of moving, joined together. Samantha Mathis may be in the center in the frame— within the logic of the film *The Thing Called Love*, its icon, and within its narrative, a symbol—but encountering her as she intones these poetic words to River Phoenix, in this moment and framed in this way, is an experience substantiated by the more elusive indexical qualities lingering around performances in the cinema. Part of the challenge she poses as a performer here is felt within the film itself, by Phoenix's character James: an immediate cut to Phoenix suggests that he does not quite know how to respond to Mathis's poetic subjectivity. After she speaks the lines from Graves, the film cuts to Phoenix, who mumbles that he thinks he knows that poem. A cut back to Mathis, still looming above him, finds her assertively telling him to "shut up," before she kisses him.

This moment reminds me that we may not yet know these poetic lines, that film lovers may still have some work to do in appreciating performance in cinema. If, as I have suggested earlier in this book, an androgynous way of looking at performance is an ideal, or at least my ideal—a way of looking which might remain sensuously open to affects from a range of performers—this is a position that cannot simply be assumed or easily performed, but which must be worked toward, a position which is perhaps itself a performance—of viewing, and of writing, and of life—that might remain always just one gesture away from full iconic or symbolic realization. I suspect I haven't reached it (most of the performers I've discussed in this book are, after all, women). But that elusiveness is what gives this ideal ongoing life, indeed what prevents it from being something as static as an ideal.

In his commentary track for the DVD of *The Thing Called Love*, Bogdanovich notes the relative paucity of close-ups in the film, underscoring his preference for long takes and shots in which two, three, or four central actors are grouped together. He makes particular reference to a shot near the end of the film, in which both River Phoenix and Dermot Mulroney are closely figured together in the frame, a moment in which the two characters are working out their desires for the Mathis character but which also contains homoerotic undertones (the observation of these undertones is mine, not Bogdanovich's; see *The Thing Called Love* DVD for the director's own observations about the scene). He states that this shot, framing the characters in an intimate close-up, is a singular example of such framing in the film. He forgets, however, not only the aforementioned close-up of Mathis as she reads the Graves poem to Phoenix but also a striking moment earlier in her performance in which her gestures edge a camera into a very close framing. After the line-dancing scene described earlier, Mathis and Phoenix have a playful argument. After some sparring and flirting, Mathis takes charge and, tiring of Phoenix's excuses, wraps her right arm around him, a gesture posed somewhere in-between an affectionate embrace and an aggressive headlock (Figure 13). Timed with her movement, the camera and Phoenix both move; as she draws Phoenix close with her gesture the camera watching her is motivated to get closer, too, now framing her, and Phoenix, in a close two-shot nearly as intimate as the one of Phoenix and Mulroney near the end of the film.

Figure 13: *The Thing Called Love* (1993).

As in my initial viewing of the film, the vivid, performative subjectivity of Samantha Mathis attracts my eye, pulling me forward just as it pulls the camera's attention forward with gestural strength. In this moment, the "obvious" content of the frame—the salient, unmistakable, fully intentional gesture of one actor—is as sublime as any marginal, contingent, or accidental detail might be. With her performance conveying both affection and playful impatience, Mathis reminds us of the ability of actors not only to enchant but also assertively confront. That Bogdanovich's film functions as the site of this encounter with a defiant and assertive subjectivity suggests the valuable way in which he channeled the tragedy surrounding the making of *They All Laughed* into the apparently more happy assemblage of *The Thing Called Love*, a film that might be understood as an extension of his musings, begun in his writing in *The Killing of the Unicorn*, on the various ways women incarnate characters in the cinema. Such an idea prompts a love for performance to account also for the ways different kinds of onscreen subjectivities, performed in a tapestry of images and visions of the everyday, might provoke even as they delight and charm.

So I end this book by reasserting the idea that performers have a special role to play in our account of film experience and its tantalizingly elusive qualities. And actors, in the end, always remain elusive, no matter how much they move us. Lloyd Michaels, in his fascinating rumination on character in film, *The Phantom of the Cinema*, observes that actors in movies, the phantoms of his title,

> continue to haunt our imagination and memory because, as mimetic representations, they reflect our unrequited desire for human contact, and because, as formal elements in a cinematic narrative, they remind us of the camera's capacity to deceive as well as to reveal. In either case, these spectral figures compel our attention by their very quality of remaining unpossessible.[70]

Despite this elusiveness, or precisely because of it, actors are essential to time spent writing on film. When the viewing self is struck by one of the darts an actor throws from onscreen, helpless infatuation need not result. Those darts can fill us instead with the energy to write about the actors who charge our experiences of cinema with unpredictable, enchanting life.

NOTES

1 James Salter, *Light Years* (London: Penguin, 2007), 33.
2 Marcel Proust, *In Search of Lost Time, Vol. 1: Swann's Way* (New York: The Modern Library, 2003), 101.
3 In his book *The Horse Who Drank the Sky: Film Experience Beyond Narrative and Theory* (New Brunswick, N.J.: Rutgers University Press, 2008), Murray Pomerance weaves a way of viewing film that pivots on the phrase "the voluptuous gaze," in which the viewer, in watching a film, looks and lingers upon moments within it with something like "the experience of phantasms"; in a voluptuous gaze, for Pomerance, viewers are attracted "*in the same way as* viewers of the cinema of attractions [during the era of early silent cinema] were opened more generally" (32). Here Pomerance makes a connection between a viewing that lingers on moments rather than one which races ahead in the consumption of plot and genre.
4 Brenda Austin-Smith reminds us in her work on acting that the decisions actors make that result in onscreen performance are never viewable, for performances are the products of "internal deliberations" to which we can never be witness. See Austin-Smith, "Acting Matters: Noting Performance in Three Films," in *Theorizing Film Acting*, ed. Aaron Taylor (London: Routledge, 2012), 19.
5 Charles Affron, in his stupendous book on film performance, discusses this fascination with the way an actor can *repeatedly* enchant: "Garbo can die for me around the clock. I can stay [with] her in that final moment of her life; I can turn off the sound and watch, turn off the picture and listen, work myriad transformations in speed and brilliance, and then restore the original without losing a particle of its integrity" (5). See Affron, *Star Acting: Gish, Garbo, Davis* (New York: E.P. Dutton, 1977).
6 Patrice Pavis, *Analyzing Performance: Theater, Dance, and Film* (Ann Arbor: University of Michigan Press, 2008), 18.
7 Roland Barthes, *Mythologies*, trans. Annette Lavers (Hill and Wang: New York, 1972), 56.
8 Jean Epstein, "The Senses I (b)," in *French Film Theory and Criticism, 1907–1939*, Vol. 1 (Princeton, NJ: Princeton University Press, 1993), 243.
9 Christian Keathley, in his work on cinephilia, discusses the power of *photogénie* and its relationship to cinephilia extensively. See Keathley, *Cinephilia and History, or the Wind in the Trees* Bloomington: Indiana University Press, 2006), 96–102. Robert B. Ray, in his writings, has also sought to resurrect *photogénie* as a concept animating film research and writing. See Ray, *How a Film Theory Got Lost, or Other Mysteries in Cultural Studies* (Bloomington: Indiana University Press, 2002), 34.

10 Daniel Varndell has written beautifully about the effects of time and nostalgia on our perception of screen performance. See "Touched by Time: Memories of the Faded Star," in *Was It Yesterday?: Nostalgia in Contemporary Film and Television*, ed. Matthew Leggatt (State University of New York Press, 2020), 51–70.

11 Alan Rudolph, correspondence with author (July 2018). I explore this performance more extensively in my book *Geraldine Chaplin: The Gift of Film Performance* (Edinburgh: Edinburgh University Press, 2020). Portions of this description of Chaplin's performance in the present text are revised variations of passages from that book.

12 See Ray, *How a Film Theory Got Lost*, 34.

13 Ray, *How a Film Theory Got Lost*, 4.

14 See, in addition to *How a Film Theory Got Lost*, *The ABCs of Classical Hollywood* (Oxford: Oxford University Press, 2008).

15 Keathley, *Cinephilia and History, or the Wind in the Trees*; see pages 168–77 for an evocative, anecdotal exploration of a cinephiliac moment involving Natalie Wood in *Rebel Without a Cause*. As a side note, Keathley prefers the spelling of "cinephiliac" in keeping with the "necrophiliac" undertones of engaging with past cinema—and, in particular, the idea that what we are seeing is a world past (see also footnote 27).

16 Rashna Wadia Richards, *Cinematic Flashes: Cinephilia and Classical Hollywood* (Bloomington: Indiana University Press, 2013).

17 See Scott Balcerzak and Jason Sperb, eds., *Cinephilia in the Age of Digital Reproduction: Film, Pleasure, and Digital Culture, Vol. 1* (London: Wallflower Press, 2009), and its follow-up by the same editors, *Cinephilia in the Age of Digital Reproduction: Film, Pleasure and Digital Culture, Vol. 2* (London: Wallflower Press, 2012).

18 Keathley, *Cinephilia and History, or the Wind in the Trees*, 45.

19 The idea of a discerning and distinctive connoisseurship, not unlike that found in the art world, is a key concept to the cinephilia theorized in Keathley, *Cinephilia and History* (see pages 15–16). "Cinephilic" uses of social media may ultimately be nothing more than the latest form this connoiseurship takes.

20 David Bordwell, Chapter 3, "Classical Narration," in Bordwell, Janet Staiger, and Kristen Thompson, *The Classical Hollywood Cinema: Film Style & Mode of Production to 1960* (New York: Columbia University Press, 1985), 31.

21 Liz Czach, "Cinephilia, Stars, and Film Festivals," in *Cinema Journal* 49, no. 2 (2010): 145.

22 Murray Pomerance, *Moment of Action: Riddles of Cinematic Performance* (New Brunswick, N.J.: Rutgers University Press, 2016), 16.

23 Chris Fujiwara, "Cinephilia and the Imagination of Filmmaking," in *Framework: The Journal of Cinema and Media* 50, nos. 1 and 2 (Spring and Fall 2009), 194

24 Jacques Rivette, "On Imagination," trans. Liz Heron, in Jim Hillier, ed., *Cahiers du Cinéma, The 1950s: Neo-Realism, Hollywood, New Wave* (Cambridge, M: Harvard University Press, 1995), 1, 104. Originally published as "De l'invention," *Cahiers du Cinéma* 27, October 1953.

25 Quoted in Richard Roud, *A Passion for Films: Henri Langlois and the Cinémathèque Française* (New York: Viking Press, 1983), 9.

26 Kenneth Tynan, "Introduction: The Girl in the Black Helmet," in *Lulu in Hollywood*, *Expanded Edition* (Minneapolis: University of Minnesota Press, 2000), ix.

27 Christian Keathley refers to the necrophiliac undertones of cinephilia in *Cinephilia and History, or the Wind in The Trees*, 38, following the cue of Paul Willemen in "Through the Glass Darkly: Cinephilia Reconsidered," in *Looks and Frictions: Essays in Cultural*

Studies and Film Theory (Bloomington and Indianapolis: Indiana University Press), 227. The tension between death and life in cinephilic viewing is also a key theme in Lesley Stern, *Dead and Alive: The Body as Cinematic Thing* (Montreal: caboose, 2012).

28 It is worth pointing out here the plethora of ways that actors can be "brought back to life," so to speak, in the twenty-first century, in the form of academic video essays (which include clips of performances from all eras of cinema), and, perhaps more perniciously, in "deepfake" videos on the internet, which reanimate departed actors in, I think, relatively dishonest, and decidedly nonacademic, ways.

29 Deborah Solomon, *Utopia Parkway: The Life and Work of Joseph Cornell* (New York: Other Press, 2015), 117.

30 Joe McElhaney, "Bess Flowers: Film Star," in *Senses of Cinema* 23 (December 2002), http://sensesofcinema.com/2002/the-female-actor/symposium1/.

31 Ibid.

32 Keathley discusses the idea of anecdotal and lightly autobiographical writing as a possible energy source for a historically situated cinephilic scholarship. See *Cinephilia and History*, 136–40.

33 James Morrison, *Auteur Theory and* My Son John (New York: Bloomsbury), 2018.

34 James Morrison, *Auteur Theory and* My Son John, 58.

35 James Morrison, *Auteur Theory and* My Son John, 25.

36 Stanley Cavell, *The World Viewed: Reflections on the Ontology of Film, Enlarged Edition* (Cambridge, Mass.: Harvard University Press, 1995), 256.

37 Stanley Cavell, *The World Viewed*, 27.

38 In her book *Beyond the Looking Glass: Narcissism and Female Stardom in Studio-Era Hollywood* (New York and Oxford: Berghahn, 2014), Ana Salzberg speculates that viewer and film stars can strike certain intimate and creative bonds of connection, not unlike the kind of intimacy afforded in close-ups, but which are not necessarily tied to the framing and position of the camera. "[I]n considering the sensory resonance of the pool scene from *The Philadelphia Story*, one could arguably build on the notion of close-up vision to consider the intimacy between viewer and star. More precisely, one could suggest that Hepburn invites a close-up *on* vision itself—a heightened awareness of the visual pleasure inspired by the actress' on-screen form as it alternately merges with and diverges from (pre)conceptions wrought by persona and conventions of the feminine ideal" (40).

39 Lesley Stern and George Kouvaros, "Introduction: Descriptive Acts," in *Falling for You: Essays on Cinema and Performance*, eds. Stern and Kouvaros (Sydney: Power Publications, 2006), 17.

40 See Nicole Brenez, *Abel Ferrara*, trans. Adrian Martin (Champaign: University of Illinois Press, 2014), 24–25.

41 Christian Keathley, *Cinephilia and History*, 53.

42 Jean-Luc Godard, *Godard on Godard*, trans. Tom Milne (New York: Da Capo Press, 1972), 29.

43 Christian Keathley, *Cinephilia and History*, 48.

44 Numerous scholars of film acting have paid close attention to these systems. Cynthia Baron, for example, has written extensively on methods and approaches to acting in various historical and industrial contexts, most recently in *Modern Acting: The Lost Chapter of American Film and Theatre* (London: Palgrave, 2016). James Naremore's classic study of *Acting in the Cinema* (Berkeley, Calif.: University of California Press, 2008), is also exemplary of such work.

45 P. David Marshall, *Celebrity and Power: Fame in Contemporary Culture* (Minneapolis: University of Minnesota Press, 2014), 17.

46 Jonathan Goldman, *Modernism is the Literature of Celebrity* (Austin: University of Texas Press, 2011), 127.

47 James Morrison, *Auteur Theory and* My Son John, 126.

48 Jean-Luc Godard, *Godard on Godard*, 39.

49 André Bazin, *What is Cinema? Volume II* (Berkeley and Los Angeles: University of California Press, 1971), 35–36.

50 V.F. Perkins, "Moments of Choice," *The Movie*, no. 58, 1141. (Reprinted in A. Lloyd, ed., *Movies of the Fifties*, London: Orbis Publishing, 1982), 209–13.

51 Andrew Klevan, *Aesthetic Evaluation and Film* (Manchester: Manchester University Press, 2018), 172.

52 Andrew Klevan, *Disclosure of the Everyday: Undramatic Achievement in Narrative Film* (Trowbridge, Wiltshire: Flicks Books, 2001), 21.

53 See James Naremore, *Charles Burnett: A Cinema of Symbolic Knowledge* (Oakland, Calif.: University of California Press, 2018), 56–57.

54 Erving Goffman, *The Presentation of the Self in Everyday Life* (Harmondsworth: Penguin, 1990).

55 Christian Keathley, *Cinephilia and History*, 95.

56 Alex Simon, "Peter Bogdanovich's Year of the Cat," in *Peter Bogdanovich: Interviews*, ed. Peter Tonguette (Jackson: University Press of Mississippi, 2015), 155.

57 This concluding section to this book is a reimagined and reworked variation of a longer essay by me on Bogdanovich, cinephilia, and performance. See Steven Rybin, "Songs of Cinephilic Life: Peter Bogdanovich's *They All Laughed* and *The Thing Called Love*," in *The Journal of Film and Video* 71, no. 3 (2019), 18–34.

58 See Paul Willemen, "Through a Glass Darkly." Philip Rosen, although not explicitly concerned with cinephilia, also offers a comprehensive study of the relationship between indexicality and death in *Change Mummified*, which engages with the work of Bazin, especially. Susan Sontag's infamous epitaph for cinema and cinephilia, "The Decay of Cinema" (1996), of course, is also notable in this line of discourse.

59 Phoenix's tragic demise is chronicled in Gavin Edwards, *Last Night at the Viper Room: River Phoenix and the Hollywood He Left Behind* (New York: Harper Collins, 2014).

60 I repeatedly hesitated before my use of the word "iconic", given the word's rampant overuse in social media culture (in which nearly everything under the sun seems to have become "iconic" for someone in some way or another). My sense is that this is now one of those words that can only take on substantive meaning in sharply defined contexts. I hope I have convinced my reader that in this book my use of this ubiquitous word is a little justified.

61 See Peter Bogdanovich, commentary track, *The Thing Called Love* DVD (Paramount Home Video, 2006).

62 Bogdanovich recounts his struggles to independently finance the film in Bill Teck's 2014 documentary *One Day Since Yesterday: Peter Bogdanovich & the Lost American Film*, which chronicles Bogdanovich's career and the aftermath of *They All Laughed* after Stratten's death.

63 Peter Bogdanovich, *The Killing of the Unicorn: Dorothy Stratten, 1960–1980* (London: Futura, 1984), 8.

64 Thomas J. Harris mentions the existence of this alternate cut (which he screened with Bogdanovich) in his book *Bogdanovich's Picture Shows:* (Metuchen, N.J.: Scarecrow Press, 1991). According to the author, one major change was the substitution of a Bruce Springsteen song ("Out on the Street") for Benny Goodman's "Sing Sing Sing," in the scene from *They All Laughed* at the roller disco rink (239).

65 *The Thing Called Love* DVD.

66 Peter Bogdanovich, *The Killing of the Unicorn*, 174.

67 Ibid., 175

68 "Two lovers" refers here both to the performers and the characters: Mathis and Phoenix became involved in a romantic relationship on the set of the film, which lasted until Phoenix's death.

69 The poem "Change" is included in the collection of poems by Robert Graves entitled *Collected Poems* (Garden City, N.Y.: Anchor Books, 1966), glimpsed in Miranda's suitcase in the hotel room scene.

70 Llloyd Michaels, *The Phantom of the Cinema: Character in Modern Film* (Albany: State University of New York Press, 1998), xv.

INDEX

400 Blows, The 27
A bout de souffle (1960) 40
Adair, Gilbert 10
Adjani, Isabelle 35–36, 40
Adler, Stella 47
Agamben, Giorgio 28
Altman, Robert 47

Balcerzak, Scott 10
Ballad of Narayama, The (1958) 19
Barthes, Roland 3, 4, 10, 15, 30, 45
Baxter, Anne 31
Bazin, André 30, 38
Beggars of Life (1928) 16
Bell, Ronnie 41
Bertolucci, Bernardo 21, 22, 26
Bill of Divorcement, A (1932) 1, 3, 11, 31
Bogart, Humphrey 44
Bogdanovich, Peter 47–49, 52–54, 56–58, 61–63, 65, 67
Bordwell, David 10, 29
Brando, Marlon 32
Brenez, Nicole 28, 29
Brooks, Louise 16
Bullock, Sandra 51, 53
Burnett, Charles 41, 45

Cahiers du cinéma 23
camera movement 2, 21, 35, 36, 66
Camille (1936) 8, 12
Camp, Colleen 57, 58
Carradine, Keith 7, 8
Cash, Johnny 62
Cassavetes, John 48
Cavell, Stanley 23–25, 30, 48
Chaplin, Charlie 32
Chaplin, Geraldine 7, 8, 11, 12

cinephilia 9, 11, 17, 23, 31, 53
Clayburgh, Jill 21
Cornell, Joseph 17, 29, 39
Crónica de un niño solo (*Chronicle of a Lonely Child* 1965) 27
Cukor, George 1, 2, 7, 8, 11
Czach, Liz 11

De Palma, Brian 47
Diary of a Lost Girl (1929) 16
Douglas, Kirk 29
Duering, Carl 35
Dwan, Allan 47

East of Borneo (1931) 17
Easter, Sally 41
editing (film technique) 1, 13, 14, 35, 38, 53, 57, 58
Edwards, Blake 56
Eisenstein, Sergei 23
Epstein, Jean 3, 4, 9, 10, 15, 45

Favio, Leonardo 27, 29
Ferrara, Abel 29
figural writing 28–31
Flowers, Bess 18–19, 23
Ford, John 47
framing (shot composition) 1, 14, 35, 66
French New Wave 15
Friedkin, William 47
Fujiwara, Chris 15

Garbo, Greta 3, 4, 7, 8, 11, 12, 15, 45
Gazzara, Ben 48, 56
Genina, Augusto 16
gesture (in performance) 1, 3, 4, 11, 12, 17, 25, 27, 31, 33, 36–45, 52, 56–58, 66
Girl I Loved, The (1946) 13–15, 19

Girl in Every Port, A (1928) 16
Godard, Jean-Luc 24, 31, 37, 38
Goldman, Jonathan 32
Grant, Cary 10
Graves, Robert 62–65
Gunning, Tom 23

Hansen, Patti 56, 58
Haskell, Molly 63
Hawks, Howard 16
Hayakawa, Sessue 3, 4, 9, 15, 45
Hepburn, Audrey 48, 56
Hepburn, Katharine 1, 2, 9, 11, 31
Hitchcock, Alfred 10
Hobart, Rose 17, 29
Holmes, Jessie 42
Honor of His House, The (1918) 3

Igawa, Kuniko 13, 19
In a Lonely Place (1950) 43, 44
indexicality 30–33

Keathley, Christian 9, 10, 30
Kemper, Dennis 42
Kinoshita, Keisuke 13–15, 19
Klevan, Andrew 44
Kouvaros, George 28

Ladd, Alan 7
Langlois, Henri 16
Les Carabiniers (1963) 24
Luna (1979) 21–22, 25, 26
Lust for Life (1956) 29

Magnificent Ambersons, The (1942) 31
Manners, David 1
Marshall, P. David 32
Martin, Adrian 28
Mathis, Samantha 51–53, 59, 62–67
McElhaney, Joe 19
Michaels, Lloyd 67
Minnelli, Vincente 29
mise en scène 1, 31, 37, 38, 46
Monroe, Marilyn 32
Morrison, James 23, 37, 38
Mulroney, Dermot 51, 66
My Brother's Wedding (1983) 43–45
My Own Private Idaho (1991) 55

Naremore, James 45
Neill, Sam 36
Nickelodeon (1976) 56
North by Northwest (1959) 10
Novak, Blaine 56, 58

Ôtsuka, Norio 14

Pabst, G.W. 16
Paisan (1946) 39
Pandora's Box (1928) 16
Pavis, Patrice 3, 4
Perkins, V.F. 43, 44
Phoenix, River 48, 49, 51, 55–56,
    63, 65, 66
photogénie 4, 9
Pomerance, Murray 12
Possession (1981) 35–36, 40
Presley, Elvis 62
Prix de Beauté (1930) 16
Pump Up the Volume (1990) 52

Ray, Nicholas 7, 15, 16, 43
Ray, Robert B. 9
Rebel Without a Cause (1955) 7
Richards, Rashna Wadia 10
Ritter, John 56, 58
Rivette, Jacques 15
Rodowick, D.N. 28
Rose Hobart (1936) 17, 39
Rossellini, Roberto 39
Rudolph, Alan 7, 8

Saint Jack (1979) 47
Scorsese, Martin 47
Shepherd, Cybill 63
Silas, Everette 41, 42, 44, 45
Skin Deep (1989) 56
Smith, Jeff 29
Soloman, Deborah 17
Sopranos, The (television series) 47
Speed (1994) 53
Sperb, Jason 10
Stern, Lesley 28
Stewart, Jimmy 9
Stratten, Dorothy 48, 49, 56–58,
    61, 64
Super Mario Bros. (1993) 52

Targets (1968) 47
They All Laughed (1981) 47, 49, 56–63, 67
Thing Called Love, The (1993) 47, 49, 51–57, 59, 60, 62–67
This is My Life (1992) 52
Thompson, Kristin 29
Truffaut, François 27
Twenty-Four Eyes (1954) 19
Tynan, Kenneth 16

Vitti, Monica 27, 30, 33, 65
voice (in performance) 1, 3, 8, 11, 41, 44

Welcome to L.A. (1976) 7–8, 11, 12
Wellman, William A. 16
What Price Hollywood? (1932) 7

Żuławski, Andrzej 35, 36, 40